THE BASICS OF INFORMATION SKILLS TEACHING

THE BASICS OF INFORMATION SKILLS TEACHING

IAN MALLEY

CLIVE BINGLEY   LONDON

© Ian Malley 1984. Published by Clive Bingley Limited,
7 Ridgmount Street, London WC1E 7AE, and printed in England by
Redwood Burn Limited, Trowbridge, Wiltshire. All rights reserved.
No part of this publication may be photocopied, recorded or
otherwise reproduced, stored in a retrieval system or transmitted
in any form or by any electronic means without the prior permission
of the copyright holder and publisher.

First published 1984

British Library Cataloguing in Publication Data

Malley, Ian
    The basics of information skills teaching.
        1. Information storage and retrieval systems —
    Study and teaching
        I. Title
        025   Z699

ISBN 0 85157 378 9

Typeset by Allset in 11 on 12 point Baskerville
2345888786

Contents

Introduction

Scope

One might surmise that since this book is being published by Clive Bingley Limited and that the primary market is the professional librarian in a small library, the use of the term 'information skills' instead of 'library skills' in the book's title is simply an attempt to take advantage of the current swell of interest in 'information' or 'information technology', and thus to engage the interest of a wider readership than library personnel alone. Not so. This book genuinely attempts to consider the vastly broader question of information skills and its teaching.

The set of information skills includes library skills, certainly, but it also includes communication skills, study skills, reading skills, and a mixture of skills which might be conveniently described as learning skills. All of these skills have one thing in common — the handling of information. Each of these skills might indeed be translated into terms like the acquisition of information, the retrieval of information, the organization of information, the interpretation of information, and the communication of information.

However, anyone who has had more than a slight contact with the teaching of communication skills or reading skills will realize that each of these skill areas individually demands much more than can be dealt with in this slim volume. No attempt is therefore made to illustrate in detail how such skills should be taught. Furthermore library and information personnel cannot be expected to teach all these skills in all their many facets: to begin with they may not have had the training to enable them to teach these skills to any great depth. Instead the intention is to illustrate how a programme of teaching information skills can be planned, assembled and executed, and how to take advantage of the opportunities for information skills teaching as they arise in the context and environment of the small library or information unit. An assumption is made throughout that the programme is not developed without the fullest support of your organization and, if possible, that contributions are made to it by appropriately skilled personnel in the organization, be they school teachers, college lecturers, etc, irrespective of who takes the initiative on initiating the programme.

Audience

This book is aimed at the small library or information unit which is trying to offer a programme of information skills teaching. It could be a small college library, a school library, a branch of a public library, or a special library. Typically it would have no more than one to three professional staff and a small stock (say, no more than 35,000 volumes). It is anticipated that such a library or information unit has several other characteristics, namely:

1 It has little money to spend on extra services.
2 Staff have a limited amount of time in which to develop new services.
3 Staff have a wide range of responsibilities.
4 Staff will have a good rapport with their users.

While some of these characteristics (eg lack of staff time) make the establishment of an information skills programme difficult, other characteristics (eg good rapport with users) are very positive assets. Good user rapport and support can offset many of the apparent disadvantages of limited resources.

Purpose

This book is intended to be a practical guide to the establishment of a programme of information skills teaching. This word 'programme' needs clarification at the outset. It does not imply a continuous, formal course of instruction, but rather a series of actions which taken together would be a consistent and coherent approach to the teaching of information skills. The form or method of your teaching programme is, as you will see from the chapter on teaching methods, a matter of your preference, your library and information sector, your local circumstances, and preferably a balance of all three.

Being simply a plan of many possible, alternative actions, no attempt has been made to lay down an ideal programme (not even for a particular sector) nor a blueprint for success. In a small library or information unit each of your circumstances will differ tremendously, much more than in a large university or polytechnic, and not even for these sectors can sensible model plans be recommended.

If you scan the contents you will see chapters on 'Programme design and planning', 'Aims and objectives', 'Users and user needs', etc and say that these belong more to the theory than to the practice of teaching information skills. This mistaken impression arises from the fact that too often information personnel rush into the preparation of programme content, teaching methods and teaching materials, taking short-cuts through what seem to be the philosophical, abstract and non-practical areas of programme planning and design. Planning and design is not only necessary, it is an integral part of the whole programme, and it should be evident at every stage of the programme from its initiation through to its implementation to its evaluation. To try to emphasize this most of the chapters following Chapter 1 on 'Programme design and planning' are designed as expansions of that chapter, and most of these subsequent chapters are not just prescriptions for action but a discussion of alternatives that have to be weighed, taking into account advantages and disadvantages.

All of this planning is admittedly time-consuming if it is done properly, and time in a small library or information unit is at a premium. But it is all the more necessary that this time is invested in planning, because an ill-conceived programme generally fails, and that is a wasted expenditure of time in a small unit. Where you can look for economies is to make use of the experience and expertise available inside and outside your organization. This applies particularly to teaching materials. Indeed it would have been a simple matter to assemble a kit of samples of teaching materials of all sorts from all sectors, giving you a number of guidelines for linking together in a series of information skills units, according to your local circumstances and needs. But the danger is that you would have ended up with what would have been a collection of isolated units on information skills and not a coherent, logical programme for the teaching of information skills.

Chapter One

Programme design and planning

Introduction
The literature of information skills teaching reveals little discussion of programme design, planning and objectives, although there is plenty on programme description, content, and teaching methods and modes. This is not entirely surprising because the planning of a programme can be a slow and tedious business. Moreover, for many the opportunity to offer a programme may come at short notice with little time for thorough planning: most of the effort then has to go into the content of the programme.

But if a programme wants the best chance of success, then a methodical, step-by-step, stage-by-stage approach is essential. This process paradoxically can, and sometimes should, mean that you may not proceed to implement the programme. Many programmes never get to the evaluation stage. The truth is that some of these should not have got to the implementation stage. In other words, they ought to have been cancelled at the planning stage. There may have been a number of circumstances which in themselves might seem small and unimportant but taken together might make the programme untenable or unacceptable. A careful, stage-by-stage approach helps to highlight these problems, and possibly even remove them at the planning stage when time and anticipation permit it.

The various stages in designing a programme of teaching information skills correspond roughly to five basic questions:
1 Why teach information skills?
2 Who is being taught?
3 Where are you going?

4 What is being taught?

5 How are the skills to be taught?

These are five essential questions and all of them must be considered and answered if a genuine attempt is to be made at designing a programme. The order in which they are posed is important. Perhaps the above order is debatable but it has a certain logic about it. Clearly, you must first ask the basic question 'why?' Then you need to know all about the audience or target group for instruction before you can decide what the objectives of the programme are. Only then can you think about what you are going to teach, and lastly you have to decide how to teach the skills.

Within the five questions just posed there are a number of other questions or problems that have to be considered which make it difficult to maintain the above order in this book. In fact the questions of 'who is being taught?' and 'where are you going?' are linked in such a way that it is convenient briefly to consider users and their needs amidst aims and objectives, and leave their fuller discussion to the following chapter.

Apart from this the order of topics in this book follows the order of the questions above. This is partly to illustrate the logic of planning and designing a programme in this way, and partly to reinforce the stage-by-stage process. Later chapters on topics like timing, cooperation and the skills you need, remain until last but remember that they weave their way in and out of programme planning. However, they can be such a problem that they are worth considering and re-emphasizing on their own.

Chapter Two

Why teach a programme of information skills?

Introduction
This chapter considers in general terms why you should or
should not have a programme of information skills teaching.
In a later chapter the question is considered in some more
detail in relation to the information user's need for information skills. Here some of the broader reasons and implications are considered.

Why should you teach a programme?
Is there anything in the library and information field which is
so inherently difficult that it requires instruction on its
retrieval, organization, evaluation, communication, etc? Have
your library and information users exhibited or expressed a
particular difficulty with the information? Have you been
approached by these people and been asked to arrange and
organize a programme? Is there any evidence that an information skills programme in your area improves information-
handling abilities?

If your answer is 'no' to all of these questions then you
should probably not proceed with a programme. It is not
really enough to claim that the acquisition of information
skills is important, and use this as sole justification for
establishing a programme. You may feel and argue that they
are important, but is your opinion shared by your information
users? Neither is it really enough to point out that programmes
of teaching information skills are common. Nor is it enough
to say that there is a vast and increasing literature on the
subject, much of it saying that it is a 'good thing'. Nor is it
enough to refer to the growing number of recommendations,
from outside as well as inside the information community,

that information skills should be part of everyone's armoury in this age of information.

What I am trying to emphasize is that not only you as library and information personnel, as well as various outside influences, must have strong reasons for establishing a programme, but your clientele, your users, must have equally strong or even stronger reasons for supporting the programme. In other words local user needs, real not perceived, must determine the establishment of an information skills programme. Otherwise, at worst the programme will be poorly attended, or at best you will get little reaction to your efforts from those attending.

Considering external factors, there is a substantial amount of research which indicates that library skills programmes do improve the information-handling abilities of library users — at least in the short term. At the same time there is, as might be expected, a substantial body of evidence that indicates that library skills programmes have no effect. So you take your pick.

As far as you are concerned in the small library or information unit there is no UK research to help you to come to a decision in those terms. You have to rely on the needs for information skills of your own users. But even then you still have to consider whether a programme of teaching information skills is the right thing to do in your situation. First of all you have to remember that such a programme is one of a number of competing information services which you can provide in a library or information unit. You cannot expect to provide all of them, and part of your managerial function will be to determine your priorities in the services you offer. Planning and implementing an information skills programme is a considerable undertaking in itself, apart from the fact that it can materially affect the use of other information services you may provide. Secondly, the provision of a programme may seem the obvious response in your situation, but it may not be the most appropriate. Careful analysis might well show that the best way to overcome library and information difficulties experienced by users in the library would be to simplify the library system procedures (for example, by improving library guiding or even improving library layout so that library guiding is almost redundant) or even to develop other parts of the library and information service (for example, expanding the reference and enquiry service). And other elements of the information skills programme could be left to personnel elsewhere in the organization.

Why not somebody else?

Why shouldn't someone else, not you, run a programme of information skills? Even when information skills meant and sometimes still does mean simply library skills, the question has always been asked. Since information skills are now interpreted in a much wider sense it is an even more valid question to ask. Are you sufficiently expert or experienced to carry a well-rounded information skills programme to a successful conclusion? Is there someone else, inside or outside your organization, who might do the job better or be more appropriate for the job?

In colleges of further and higher education, where probably the greatest number if not the widest range of information skills needs to be taught, the question of 'whose responsibility?' is at its most complex. Librarians in this sector often have a dual role: firstly, it is to provide a professional library service; and secondly, it is sometimes to teach in the parent organization in part of the curriculum, usually General Studies, Liberal Studies, Communication Studies, or some such title. The latter can include elements of information skills. Thus the tutor-librarians, as they are generally known in this sector, could have the opportunity, and as far as their teaching duties are concerned, the responsibility for organizing a broadly-based information skills programme. With the advantage that they are recognized as teachers by both students and other teaching staff, they and thus the information skills programme will have some status in all eyes. Furthermore, the tutor-librarians have the advantage of a sound knowledge of the needs of the curriculum and the information needs of the students.

In many colleges, aspects of information skills like study and communication skills are accorded such importance that some teaching staff are appointed as specialists in these subjects. They are perceived as the experts at least in the acquisition and communication of information, and might even want to assume the further responsibility of teaching information skills.

In schools a similar situation to the colleges may sometimes arise. Instead of having a professional librarian whose sole function is to run the school library one could have a teacher-librarian with an added teaching role which might include some study skills teaching. At the same time more study skills instruction might be found in any one of a number of situations: for example, as part of the pastoral system, through the curriculum, as part of English studies, and so on. The question of 'whose responsibility?' can often be even more complicated in those schools when there is no agreed policy towards study skills, communication skills and other learning skills, and decisions on responsibility vary from year to year.

In special libraries or information units the question of 'whose responsibility?' is much less complicated because of the limited range of information skills that are appropriate in these organizations, which are not often avowedly educational establishments. The conflict here is not within the organization, but it is the choice between bringing in outside expertise for certain information skills instruction (or possibly sending the organization's personnel out to have them taught). On-line information retrieval skills is a common example. Most database producers and some host system operators offer programmes of on-line training for end-users and intermediaries alike. Is the best policy to send the end-user to these training programmes, or is it better to send the intermediaries to be trained, and hence give them the responsibility of training the end-users in house?

In public libraries the dilemma is somewhat different. Since in any one local authority the public library and the school are ultimately funded by the same source, and on occasions the public library may have executive responsibility for the school library service, the teaching of information skills may automatically devolve upon the public librarian. Should it do so? Can it effectively do so? Is the public librarian too remote from the school curriculum to prepare properly a full information skills programme?

But whatever the circumstances in different sectors and in different organizations, ideally the responsibility for teaching the information skills programme should be a joint one. Information skills as it is defined here is a balance of a range of skills associated with information. In toto, information skills are so varied and all-pervasive that we have no right to expect that any one party can cope with the teaching of all of them. It seems more reasonable to say that you will be involved in a major or minor role in the teaching of information skills, and the extent of your participation will depend on your wish to be involved, your competency, the politics of your environment, and sometimes your opportunism. Even in the teaching of simple library skills in higher education, the best programmes have always been a joint effort between librarian and teaching staff: the former to provide the expertise on the totality of information sources and the retrieval of information from them, and the latter to ensure that only the sources that are relevant to the student at any time are taught. A somewhat different division of labour is envisaged in this book, but a partnership is assumed nevertheless.

Chapter Three

The politics of information skills teaching

Although you can never fully anticipate the implications of establishing a programme, you should make yourself aware of some of the political problems that may arise from your initiative. Your clientele may have a limited idea of your potential as an information unit, but it may have a clear idea of the limits in which you should operate. For example, it may recognize that you have a service role, but reject a role for you which is avowedly and actively educational. In other words it may accept that you have a role as an information provider, but it may be unwilling to agree to your role in educating the clientele in the independent use, and also the effective use of information. Why do these objections arise — and how do you counter them?

Firstly, there may be a concern that setting up a programme may be to the detriment of the remainder of the service — it could overstretch manpower resources or it could stimulate and thus overload other parts of the services. These are valid arguments, so how do you counter them?

In the first case, you have to acknowledge that you are most unlikely to get additional staff to carry out your programme, even though you may have assistance from within your organization. Therefore, an existing service may have to be sacrificed in whole or in part. If so, your clientele must be made aware of this and be agreeable to this. You could argue in terms of necessity: for example, it is impossible to run a full information service for all the clientele — a proportion of the clientele must learn to be independent information users. Alternatively, you could argue in terms of personal benefits to the clientele or of benefits to the service (hence the clientele). The first approach is confrontational, the second approach is negotiable and more reasonable.

In the second case, your programme should certainly stimulate the demand and use of other services and resources. It is a double-edged sword. If it doesn't, then this may be one measure of the failure of your programme. It it does, you have to be prepared for and accept increased demand and use, but, if your programme is careful and balanced, you should expect more intelligent and effective use of existing services.

A second objection to your programme may arise from the feeling that you are stepping outside your specified role. Your appointment was almost certainly made to help provide an information service, rather than to teach, and if you are working in an educational establishment particularly, then this may be regarded with some concern. Fortunately, in the educational sector it is more easy to justify some element of teaching because basically the institution's prime task is to teach and educate. Nevertheless even here the case has to be argued for the inclusion of the teaching of information skills as part of information service provision.

Thirdly, there may be the feeling that not only are you stepping out of your role as service provider, but that you are stepping into someone else's territory, intentionally or otherwise. In some establishments, especially in colleges of further and higher education and in schools, this can be a difficult obstacle. It has also been made a much harder obstacle in recent years as the concept of information skills has changed from simply being concerned with library skills to something incorporating aspects of study skills and other related skills. In schools, for example, this new scope of information skills will impinge on classroom teaching — and in two ways: firstly, and correctly so, on the learning habits of the pupils: and secondly, on the teaching of a number of study skills by the teacher. Teachers may or may not relish this extension of the role of the librarian in this respect. In the colleges of further and higher education, the situation is even more sensitive because there are often lecturers appointed primarily and largely to teach study and communication skills, eg in courses variously titled Liberal Studies, General Studies, etc. From their point of view an informal programme covering library orientation and certain library skills might not be considered a threat, but any move towards a formal programme which includes the communication of information, etc might be unacceptable.

Fourthly, there may be the suspicion that your programme of teaching information skills, and your role in it, might be used as a lever for enhancement of status or salary. In colleges of further and higher education some years ago such a tactic by the librarian might have borne fruit, but it would be quite unrealistic for a librarian to expect such a reward now. Rather the situation is that those who are on a teaching grade (eg the Burnham scale) are having difficulty in retaining this grade. Perhaps in a small way programmes on the teaching of information skills do help to preserve the status, but very rarely has such teaching the standing that it might or might not decide employment grades.

In the last resort, the most effective way of countering the above objections is to make your clientele, your associates in the organization, as well as the ultimate authority in your organization, aware of what you intend and what you are doing at every stage of development of the programme — both on paper and in person. The best opportunity is at the planning stage, when aims and objectives are set. Later, in my discussion of programme aims and objectives, compatibility with all other interested parties' aims and objectives in the organization is stressed. It should also be stressed in this context as the most effective solution in countering the problems of the politics of these programmes. Not all of the problems arise through misunderstandings and poor communication, but good liaison can reduce the number of difficult and sensitive situations.

Chapter Four

Aims and objectives

Introduction
Even in information skills programmes where there is some semblance of design and planning, the formal setting of aims and objectives is often neglected. There are various reasons for this, but primarily the answer lies in the differing attitudes of those running the programmes.

For some it is philosophically unacceptable because it is presupposed that the setting of aims and objectives may pre-determine what is taught and thus restrict the learning possi-bilities of the learner. For these people, therefore, it is too restrictive and rigid. Others, however, like to plan a programme systematically, judging that well thought-out objectives will give the programme a purpose, structure and coherence. In practice, the first group often has a number of aims and objectives which are subconsciously held but never made explicit, and the second group often compromises its aims and objectives as the programme proceeds.

For many others it is the practical problem of setting aims and objectives that results in their exclusion from programme planning. The argument is that they are both difficult and time-consuming to prepare. This chapter attempts to show that this is not necessarily so. But first of all consider the arguments for and against.

The arguments for and against setting objectives
There are two main arguments against the setting of objectives.

Firstly, it is argued that the statement of explicit objectives brings a rigidity and inflexibility to the teaching programme: that is, the detailed statement of objectives is a constraining influence on educational innovation. This can be the case, but it need not be; it will be so if individual objectives are not modified, removed or added when changed circumstances demand it: for example, in the light of student reaction or interim evaluation. Objectives once set are not sacrosanct. A set of objectives determines a particular line of action, but if a new line of action seems to be required then this can be incorporated in a new set of objectives.

Secondly, since many programmes of information skills teaching are not formally taught, it is regarded as inappropriate to state precise objectives. However, students, for example, involved in an informal or self-learning programme, probably would appreciate a *framework* for learning, and the various objectives could provide this framework.

There are five main arguments for the setting of objectives.

Firstly, setting objectives and actually putting them down on paper brings a discipline and structure to the planning of the programme.

Secondly, they will help you to justify your programme to those in the organization of which you are part. Your programme is going to use some of the resources of your organization (be they financial or otherwise) so at the very least you will be asked what you are trying to do. A statement of objectives, especially if it is well-constructed, shows that the programme has been carefully thought out.

Thirdly, objectives help you to determine the content of the programme more easily, selecting what is necessary, as opposed to what is merely desirable and even superfluous in the programme. If you have a constant reminder of what the user should be able to do at the end of the programme, then it is easier to determine the means to the end. This will become more apparent later in this chapter.

Fourthly, articulating objectives gives a direction to the programme that will ultimately and almost automatically lead to easier management of the evaluation process. Quite simply, if you lay out precisely what you or your users intend to do at the beginning it is relatively easy to measure at the end of the programme if you have succeeded. This is only part of the evaluation process but it is an important one. Furthermore, objectives can pinpoint weaknesses in the programme, if evaluation indicates that certain objectives are not met. Perhaps the objectives were wrong, perhaps the teaching methods and modes were at fault, but some weakness somewhere becomes apparent.

Fifthly, setting the objectives and showing them to the target audience for the programme gives them a direction. In other words the group knows where it is going and knows when it has got there. Apart from the fact that the group will normally appreciate being taken into your confidence, there are two other possible advantages: namely, they might be able to complete the programme by themselves, or at least with minimal support; and it is possible at every stage for the individuals in the group to make some evaluation of their progress.

But whether you are for or against setting aims and objectives for your programme, it is important to be aware that either your target group (and any group associated with it) or even your organization itself may have clear aims and objectives; not necessarily on information skills, but perhaps on teaching and education in general. You need to discover what their respective aims and objectives are, and if they have any which relate to or impinge on yours. *The aims and objectives of your programme must be compatible with the aims and objectives of theirs.*

Even if the other parties have no stated aims and objectives, you should still make them aware of yours and get agreement on their acceptability. Underlying the success or failure of any programme of information skills teaching is an important and fundamental point: if there is a mismatch in aims and objectives between any of the parties involved in the programme, there is unlikely to be a successful outcome to the programme. This should be a sufficiently strong reason on its own for establishing sets of aims and objectives.

Bad and good objective setting

Some library and information personnel do attempt to set objectives, but the objectives suffer from two common faults. Firstly, they are usually a mixture of general aims and goals and one or two specific objectives. Secondly, they are usually a mixture of (primarily) librarians' objectives, students' objectives, and academic or teaching objectives — and some would not be acceptable to all parties.

Look at the following selection which has been culled from a variety of sources in higher education:

1 To enable the student to use the library effectively

2 To enable the student to study effectively
3 To develop the student's ability to find out and process information. Specifically, the student will be able to
   (a) plan and implement an efficient search strategy using library, campus and other information systems as appropriate
   (b) locate, evaluate and select appropriate materials
4 Upon leaving the university the student would measurably understand: major physical arrangements of the library (the classification and cataloguing systems); major tools of reference such as indexes and abstracts in general and specifically those in his area of study.
5 To show the students the relationship of the library to their courses and other college activities
6 To assist students to make the most effective use of materials appropriate to their assignments and course work.

All of the above are worthy and commendable, but allowing for the fact that they are taken from the environment of higher education, would they be as acceptable to those on your programme of information skills or to teaching staff or to other personnel in your organization, as they are to you? Are some of them not too vague and imprecise? And what are the criteria of success or performance for these various objectives?

If you accept the simple statement that an objective is a description of the intended result of your instruction, then to some extent the above objectives are acceptable, but as you go on to plan the programme in detail you would quickly find that they are too vague. Those above also show that you can easily get a mixture of broad and specific objectives. The ordering and classification of objectives from broad to specific is necessary in a disciplined programme.

Probably the best assistance for librarians in preparing goals and objectives is a document by Morris and Webster 'Developing objectives for library instruction'.[1] It is upon their work that the remainder of this chapter is based.

It is important to note that their development of objectives takes place within a broad strategy for setting up an information skills programme. In fact in this chapter the 'goals and objectives' elements of this strategy are just four elements within six which go to make up the analysis stage of a programme planning schedule (see Figure 1). The two elements of 'audience' and 'needs of audience' are barely touched upon in this chapter, and they are treated in more detail in the next chapter on 'Users and user needs'.

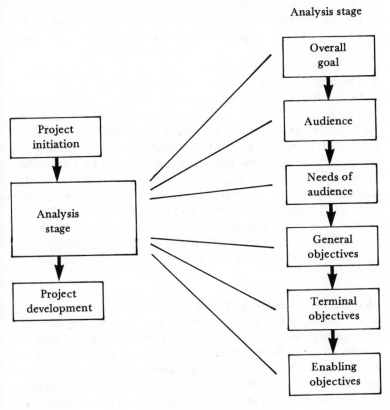

Figure 1

The overall goal of the programme

Determining the overall aim of the programme is to ask yourself the questions 'Where are we now?' and 'Where do we want to be by the time the programme is completed?'

Let's take the hypothetical case of pupils in a secondary school. For them the overall goal might be as follows:

'Pupils at secondary school X will have the information skills necessary for independent study by the time they leave school.'

This goal can be broken down into a number of simple components:

1 The broad population target
  (ie pupils at secondary school X)
2 The broad description of activities which the population
  target should be able to demonstrate
  (ie the information skills necessary for independent study)
3 The setting of a general level of competency for these
  activities
  (ie as school leavers)
4 The statement of the time scale involved
  (ie by the time they leave school).

Having put forward this goal, two further important questions
have to be asked (both of which were discussed earlier):
firstly, is it compatible with the overall goals of (a) the school,
(b) the teachers, (c) the pupils, and (d) the library? Secondly,
with adequate resources, is this programme goal reachable?
To answer these two questions you need to know, in this
case, the teachers, the pupils, and the curriculum really well
in terms of their aims and objectives; and you need to know
just what resources are available to you and your programme.
These are neither small nor easy tasks, but they have to be
done.

Identify the potential audience
Now you might argue that the target population for your
programme has just been identified when you determined the
overall goal of the programme, ie pupils at secondary school
X, in our example. In a broad sense it has, but you will
probably have to settle for only a proportion of the pupils in
the school in your proposed programme. For example, you
may not have sufficient resources (a point that has to be
ascertained in determining the goal) to cover all the pupils —
an extremely likely situation; you may find that not all the
teachers are prepared to involve their pupils in your programme. Therefore although your overall goal is still valid in the
long term, you cannot expect to cover the whole population
immediately, but you have to try and identify the most
accessible groups.

The whole question of identifying users and their information needs is much more complicated than the brief points
being made here, and the question will be considered in much
more detail in the next chapter. But it is important to see the
question of the user and his needs in the context of writing

down aims and objectives, because they are inextricably linked.

This stage of identifying the potential audience is the first in the process of narrowing and focusing your attention on to what is possible and acceptable in the programme.

Identify the information needs of your target group

This is without doubt the most important stage in designing a programme. The question will be fully explored in the next chapter and it will also regularly appear in other parts of the book.

This step is largely about relevance. There are many different information skills that can be taught in your programme, but obviously not all of them will be relevant to your target group; and even those that are ultimately relevant may not be so at any one time. Take, for example, the pupils at secondary school X: teaching first-year pupils at the school the higher-level skills of evaluating the contents of books is possibly irrelevant to those who are leaving school at sixteen, and even those who intend to go on into higher education at the end of their sixth year will probably not appreciate these skills at that stage.

The aim at this stage is to identify the specific needs of a specific group at a particular time. Briefly you need to find out
1 What skills do they already have?
2 What skills do they need to acquire?
A variety of possible methods can be used to get this information, eg questionnaires, consultation, observation, tests, etc.

Write general objectives

You have now identified a specific group for your programme and their specific needs for information skills. It is at this point that you are beginning to look in detail at the composition of the programme. The general objectives reflect this. They may seem very similar to the overall aim of the programme, but a specific sub-section of the possible audience for the programme has been targeted, and these general objectives also deal with a shorter duration of time. The general objectives deal with the objectives that will be reached by the end of the programme.

If we continue with our example of secondary school X we might now make a statement of general objectives as follows:

'First-year pupils at secondary school X should, by the end of the first year, have the necessary information skills to plan, research and write class assignments and projects at a level acceptable to their teachers.'

This is what they should have achieved by the end of the programme.

As with the statement of overall aims the general objective can be broken down into a number of components:

1 The specific population target
  (ie first-year pupils at secondary school X)
2 The broad description of activities which the population target should be able to demonstrate
  (ie have the necessary information skills to plan, research and write class assignments and projects)
3 The setting of a general level of competency for these activities
  (ie at a level acceptable to their teachers)
4 The statement of the time-scale involved
  (ie by the end of the first year)

Each of the above components is essential in the statement of the general objective, just as they were in the statement of the overall goal, and just as they will be in the statement of the terminal and enabling objectives. Each can be shortened to, respectively, target, action (the performance by the target of what he or she will be able to do), criterion (the standard of acceptable performance), and conditions (under which the performance is to take place). Thus the general objective is a statement of action, the criteria which will be regarded as acceptable performance, and the conditions under which this action takes place.

By the end of this stage you are beginning to think in terms of the programme content; that is, the skills that need to be taught to particular groups. Detailed discussion of content must be delayed for fuller treatment in a later chapter.

Write terminal objectives

A terminal objective is the behaviour (or the skill) which you expect your target to demonstrate upon the termination of a unit of instruction (or part of your programme). It is more specific than the general objective, and it also helps the target to meet the general objective. In fact the completion of several terminal objectives permits the general objective to be achieved, or in other words the general objective is made up of several more specific terminal objectives.

For example, take the case of our first-year pupils at secondary school X. The action that they will achieve if the general objective is to be met will be to 'have the necessary information skills to plan, research and write class assignments and projects'. This action can be broken down into a number of skills, for example, literature search strategies, note-taking from books, or report-writing.

You may decide to devote two hours of your total programme to each one of these information skills. Going back to the definition of a terminal objective, you can see that each of the above skills are skills which you expect your target to demonstrate upon the termination of a unit of instruction. For each one therefore you now need to write a terminal objective. For example,

'At the end of the two-hour unit on literature search strategies first-year pupils at secondary school X, given a suitable topic, should be able to retrieve enough relevant information from the library's reference book collection to handle an essay assignment on that topic.'

As with the statements of overall aims and general objectives, the terminal objective can be broken down into a number of components:

1 The specific population target
(ie first-year pupils at secondary school X)
2 The description of activities which the target group should be able to demonstrate
(ie given a suitable topic, should be able to retrieve information)
3 The setting of a level of competency for these activities
(ie enough information from the library's reference book collection to handle an essay assignment in that topic)
4 The statement of time-scale involved
(ie at the end of the two-hour unit on literature search strategies).

Write enabling objectives

If the terminal objective is the behaviour or the skill which you expect your target group to demonstrate upon termination or completion of a unit of instruction, then the enabling objectives represent the knowledge or skills that must be mastered if the target group is to attain these terminal objectives. To put it at its most simple: if you want your target group to acquire literature search strategies (this is the terminal objective) then they have to learn how to search reference books like *Encyclopaedia Britannica*, the *Oxford dictionary of quotations*, etc (these are the enabling objectives). Following from that it is clear that several enabling objectives are necessary to attain a terminal objective.

The rigour that was necessary with the other objectives is also necessary with enabling objectives, so as an example of an enabling objective we might have

'At the end of the two-hour unit on literature search strategies first-year pupils at secondary school X will be able to use *Encyclopaedia Britannica* to provide an agreed number of references for an essay assignment.'

Once again the objective can be broken down into a number of components:

1 The specific population target
 (ie first-year pupils at secondary school X)
2 The description of activities which the target group should be able to demonstrate
 (ie they will be able to use *Encyclopaedia Britannica*)
3 The setting of a level of competency for these activities
 (ie to provide an agreed number of references for an essay assignment)
4 The statement of the time-scale involved
 (ie at the end of the two-hour unit on literature search strategies).

Conclusion

With the writing of enabling objectives the analysis stage of the programme is complete — a stage which is a progression of focusing and re-focusing on specifics. This chapter has been concerned primarily with aims and objectives, the other parts of the analysis stage will be dealt with in the next chapter on user needs.

If at times you have been frustrated by the tedium and

elaborateness in the refinement of the various aims and objectives, then with some reflection you will see that you should now have a more enlightened idea of the target groups, their information skills needs and the necessary information skills, once the objectives have been set. Certainly the formulation of the foregoing general, terminal and enabling objectives should give you a much clearer picture of the total programme than any bare statement of objectives such as 'to enable the student to study effectively' or 'to enable the student to use the library effectively' can do. You should now have a clear idea of how these vague objectives can be met, and, in the case of the examples given here, how learning to use *Encyclopaedia Britannica* fits into the scheme of learning search strategies necessary for secondary school assignments. But even more important the first-year pupil and his or her teacher will also have a clear picture of the structure of the programme, and in particular of the required action, performance, the standards of acceptable performance and the conditions under which the performance is to occur at every stage.

One can of course be even more specific than we were here. For example, many statements of enabling objectives would include more precise criteria for acceptable performance: that is, introducing quantitative measures of acceptable performance. For example, getting three out of five correct references means that you have achieved the objective, but one out of five correct would mean that you had failed to meet the objective. If at the evaluation stage of your programme you are going to concentrate on quantitative assessment of success or failure then this is fine, but if not then this extra dimension should be avoided.

The statements of objectives in the way they have been done here, taken together with the knowledge of the users and their information skills needs, are sufficient for you to develop a programme which will respond to the needs of your target groups, cutting out desirable but non-essential elements or skills.

Reference

1 Morris, Jacquelyn M and Webster, Donald F *Developing objectives for library instruction.* Syracuse, New York Library Instruction Clearinghouse, 1976.

Chapter Five

Users and user needs

Introduction
This is the age of information — or so it has recently been argued. It might be more appropriately described as the age of information technology. Nevertheless it is an age when we are being bombarded with ever-increasing quantities of information, made more accessible by information technology perhaps, and occasionally better organised by information technology. We quickly and naturally learn how to adapt to and learn the use of the new technology, but gradually there is a realization that if we don't learn to use the information itself effectively we will be overwhelmed by it.

That might seem sufficient argument to justify the need for everyone to acquire information skills and consequently for us to justify an information skills programme. It is a good philosophical argument, but it is insufficient to merit setting up programmes of teaching information skills. After all we are, as a species, fairly adept at handling information. David Attenborough, in his television spectacular 'Life on earth', remarked that the characteristic that marked us (homo sapiens) out as different from all previous species was our ability to organize and store information and hence to communicate it and re-use it. If we accept this view of ourselves, then we are already fairly proficient information-handlers. So who needs programmes of teaching information skills?

The object of this chapter is to look at specific groups of our species (or at least those that cross the thresholds of libraries and information units) and investigate which of their innate information-handling skills require development, improvement or simply sharpening-up.

The identification of users

Before any attempt is made to identify the information skills needs of the users of your library or information unit, it is necessary to find out who they are, what they are doing in the organization, whether they fall into recognizable groups, how many are in the groups, etc. In other words you need to build up descriptive profiles of your users. Why is all this necessary?

Primarily, you need to know your users, their numbers, their groups, etc so that you can make a rough, preliminary choice of which section of your users you should target for your programme. If you believe strongly in the necessity and importance of having information skills, then you will probably feel that anyone and everyone within the scope of your organization should acquire these skills. Although this is a commendable ideal, it is unlikely to be a realistic one, particularly in a small library, and you will have to recognize that you must settle for perhaps only a small segment of your potential targets. At any one time you will find that some groups are more (or less) accessible, amenable and available than others. It may be possible for you to alter the odds in your favour in terms of accessibility, amenability and availability, but generally you will have to rely on opportunity and good timing.

Secondly, knowing your users means that you will know more about your organization, and from a resource point of view this is highly desirable.

Thirdly, you need to know as much as possible about each and every discernible group of users in the organization before you look at the need for information skills in any one group. Many of these groups will have some sort of relationship with one another, and the activities of one group might significantly affect the information needs of the other. To illustrate, consider a special library in a hospital. You have identified the group 'doctors'. They appear to be heavy users of the library and a wide range of information sources in it, and there are some indications that they might need some instruction in medical information sources. But what you might not have guessed, unless you had identified the group 'secretaries' and built up some profile of this group, was that the secretaries generally did all the searching and fetching on behalf of the doctors. Your energies might then be better directed to the secretaries instead of the doctors.

Building up these user group profiles could be an enormous task if it had to be done from scratch, but fortunately much of the information has already been gathered. Data and other information may have been collected on behalf of the organization for other purposes, and it may be readily available to you. For example, in colleges of higher and further education there is information on the numbers of full-time and part-time students, the numbers of students in each course in each year, the teaching responsibilities of the various teaching staff, etc. Add to this the information systematically and unsystematically gathered by the college library in the course of its day-to-day running of an information service, then there could be a substantial amount of information to draw upon.

In some sectors the detailed information you need will be relatively easy to collect, as in the case of colleges and schools. It could be less easy in the various special libraries, and in the public libraries it is usually very difficult indeed. But it is easier in all sectors provided that you inform others in the organization of the purpose of the collection, and remind yourself of the purpose for which the information is being collected — to determine which groups are most accessible, amenable and available for a programme of instruction, and above all to determine the information skills needs of those in need of a programme.

One could generalize and say that in most sectors the groups comprise students/pupils, teachers/lecturers, administrative staff, technical staff and other ancillary staff like secretaries. Many of these groups vary considerably in size from sector to sector, and sometimes they form important sub-groups, and often they differ enormously in their characteristics. It is appropriate therefore to consider briefly each sector separately — school, colleges, public libraries and special libraries. These are only guidelines to the groups you need to investigate — each organization is different in terms of its users and their needs.

Users in schools
The two main target groups in schools are obviously pupils and teachers. But within these two groups, there are a

number of sub-groups (even amongst the teachers) who have
to be identified.

Basically the pupils can be grouped by year or by form,
by ability, and, mostly at a later stage, by subject. This can
give you groups like first-year pupils through to sixth-form
pupils, those who will proceed to higher education, those
who will leave school at sixteen, those who are attending
remedial classes, those who are specially-gifted and receiving
special tuition, and so on. For some the need for a wide
range of skills is evident, for some the need for a very narrow
range of information skills is very pressing. Fortunately
the amount of information to enable you to build up descriptive profiles is vast and usually well-organized, if not always
easily accessible. But there ought to be enough available
to you on each group to help you establish an order of
priorities.

Most of your information will be provided by the teachers
who themselves could be targets for instruction, because
very few teacher-training colleges provide adequate instruction
in information skills — not formally anyway.

Within the broad range of teachers there are specialists,
perhaps in reading skills, media skills, study skills, communication skills, etc, all of which are part of the information
skills domain. You need to work in close association with
them of course. They may be thin on the ground, but there
are more substantial groups whose responsibilities in pastoral
care and administration are sufficient to mark them out as
significant groups. Their importance is not so much as
target groups for instruction, but as cooperative groups. In
schools more than any sector the support, association and
cooperation of teacher groups with functions that are fully
or partly concerned with information skills is absolutely
vital. No programme of information skills is possible without
them.

Users in colleges
The main groups in the colleges are essentially the same as
those in schools — students and teachers. Here, however, the
students can be grouped somewhat differently. The first
division is into full-time and part-time students, the latter
being usually a substantial proportion of the total student
number, and more importantly an often neglected one in

terms of library and information attention. All the students are then grouped by year, but also this time by subject. Whereas only in the latter part of the pupil's school career does subject specialization begin to emerge, the college student is usually firmly fixed in one subject or another.

As far as the teacher groups are concerned, in general the same groups as in schools are to be found. There are specialist lecturers in departments described variously as liberal studies, communication studies and general studies, who teach elements of information skills and whose cooperation you should seek. Other lecturer groups in their own specialist groups might be targets for instruction but their principal value is to provide information about the student groups.

Other groups in this sector might be technicians, administrative staff, and secretarial staff, who have information skills in their own right, but also sometimes provide information support to the lecturing staff.

Users of public libraries
In theory the range of users of public libraries is unlimited, and in theory you have an unlimited number of potential targets for your information skills programme. In practice, one public library once attracted to its library skills course the following:
1 An Open University student
2 A middle school teacher
3 A technician from a technical college
4 Three local history students
5 A school pupil attending with parent
6 Two secretaries
Three points arise from this example. Firstly, they illustrate the wide range of potential groups. Secondly, some of these people are not being catered for in their working or studying environments. Thirdly, the public library has something to offer in information skills training.

With such a diversity it is impractical to draw up lists of target groups and to decide which should have priority. Yet there are four fairly well defined groups which could be considered. They are local schoolchildren, local small businessmen, Open University students, and adult learners (for example, those attending adult education or adult literacy courses). Since public library services should be evenly

accessible to all, you cannot reasonably establish which group
should have priority for your attention, although since the
Open University students probably have their needs catered
for to some extent through that institution (especially through
their Course Units), then they might be given a lower priority.
But it is important to remember that public librarians should
be responsive to local circumstances and all local groups,
whether they be organized — classes of adult literacy students — or not organized — an ethnic minority.

The main difficulty with the users in public libraries, even
when you have targeted a group, is to get enough information about them on which to base your programme.

Users in special libraries

Without specifying a particular type of special library it is
difficult to identify and enumerate the many different types
of users of special libraries. In this, however, I have in mind
the small company or industrial library, an information unit
which you might think is in more need of a blueprint for
survival than a programme of information skills instruction.
Yet strangely enough the information skills programme in
this type of library or information unit could be just that
blueprint.

At any rate the users are grouped into management at all
levels (including library and information personnel), administrative staff, technicians, researchers and ancillary staff. If
it is well managed (and in particular if the information service
is well managed) then all the data on the various target
groups should be full and accessible.

The identification of user needs

Having identified the various groups within your organization
and formed a descriptive profile on each one, you should be
able to make a preliminary selection of those who might be
most 'susceptible' to a programme of information skills. This
selection is provisional because until you investigate the
information skills needs of the different groups you cannot
fully determine which group or groups should have priority.
It is the needs of the user that override all other consider-
ations in an information skills programme (as indeed they
should in any library and information service).

Of course by the time you have built up these group profiles you will already have a good picture of their information use and their information needs. But what you probably will not have, and this is what you really need, is the insight into their information *skills* needs.

No matter how strongly you believe in the need for a programme of information skills teaching, you should try to determine, from your users, first of all, if there is a real need for the programme, and secondly, what precisely is the nature of the need. Without careful analysis of needs, the programme has only a marginal chance of success. Even if you have been invited, say, as a librarian in a school library by a teacher to run a programme of library skills for the children in her class, it is wise to ask why the invitation has been made and what precisely is required. Does the teacher simply think that 'library skills are a good thing'? Does the teacher just want somewhere to park his or her children for an hour a week? Has he or she really thought about what the children need at that particular time? You would do well to pursue these and other questions before rushing to accept any invitation.

It is worth emphasizing the word 'real'. Too many programmes are based purely on 'perceived' needs; ie the needs of the user as perceived by information personnel. The perception of information personnel is acceptable provided it is balanced by the real needs shown implicitly and explicitly by the users and those associated with them.

For all sectors in the library and information world there exist many, many studies of users and their needs. For example, we have:

1 Studies which investigate the use made of information services and sources
2 Studies which extrapolate from the above the user's need for information services and sources
3 Studies which investigate the needs for information skills.
Most of the studies fall into the first category, fewer deal with the second, and it is very hard to find anything at all in the third category.

Consider the studies in the first category. If the study says that the services or sources are under-used, it does not necessarily mean that information skills will improve that use. Many other factors determine use and under-use, and the solution may be anything but a programme of information skills.

Studies in the second category often contain questions like 'Do you think information skills are important?' and 'Would you like a programme of information skills instruction?' The mere fact of posing such questions is likely to elicit a positive response, and once again to base your programme on this sort of information would be unwise. That is not to say that studies of use or information needs are necessarily irrelevant to information skills needs. They are only two sources of evidence you need when thinking about a programme.

Yet the major failing of these studies, unless they have been conducted within your organization, is that they are external. This is not to denigrate the value of studies in other institutions and to claim that they are inapplicable and invalid in your organization. It is simply to say that knowledge of local needs should form the bulk of your evidence for a programme.

There are several approaches to getting this evidence — consultation with your users and related group, observation of the information skills of your users, and testing the information skills of your users.

Testing information skills is a technique which is sometimes found in the schools sector and occasionally in colleges. But with this approach what is being tested is usually knowledge of information sources, and not necessarily information skills. Constructing tests to assess the latter is not at all easy. Observation of the information skills of your users is perceived to be more easy, if (usually) less systematic. In a small library or information unit the opportunities for such an approach are good.

The third possibility is consultation with your users and related groups. Avoiding the naive questions like 'would you like a programme of instruction skills?' and being wary of the replies you get to questions like 'are you having a problem?'. it is possible to get some insight into their need for information skills.

Information coming from groups associated with your target groups may be even more enlightening, because they may be more aware of the information skills problems of the target groups themselves. This particularly applies, for example, to teachers' appreciation of the information skills problems of their pupils.

It is now time to return to the specific sectors already considered, namely, schools, colleges, public libraries and special libraries, and consider the needs of particular groups for information skills instruction. Clearly, having just emphasized the necessity to beware of perceived needs, the necessity of making local needs paramount, etc I have to stress that these can be only *suggestions and generalizations* of where the information skills needs lie.

User needs in schools
The main group in this sector is the 'pupil' group, which as we have seen can be divided up by year, by level of ability, and so on. It is with this group that the fullest range of information skills can justifiably be taught.

The first point to make is that most of us spend about twelve to fourteen years of our lives as pupils in school, being taught and, hopefully, learning. If information skills have any significance in our lives, then they need to be acquired during this lengthy, formative period.

One alternative definition of information skills is learning to learn, and one of the strongly-held tenets of a large number of educationalists and teachers is that the prime purpose of education in school (and in higher education as well) is to learn how to learn, that is, to acquire a range of skills which in later life will enable us to manage new information, new experiences, etc. One could go on to further arguments which support the justification of information skills instruction, and the need would become more and more irrefutable, but these are philosophical and theoretical arguments, and what you need is something more practical.

In spite of the variety of groups and categories of pupils, one of the pupils' most enduring tasks is the completion of assignments. They may vary in complexity as pupils move through school, but the assignment technique is valid at all stages. It is on the peg of assignments (as it was and still is in higher academic institutions) that the best opportunity and environment for acquiring information skills has been hung. An assignment embodies a number of steps which approximately correspond to the whole set of information skills. Thus the assignment is a vehicle for information skills instruction as well as its justification.

The general opinion is that assignments are not performed

well and it is argued consequently that if pupils were taught information skills they would be able to perform assignments better. What you need to know if you are in the schools sector is if assignments are being done well in your school. If they are not, then you have some justification for your programme of information skills.

Some would argue that the quality of assignment work would improve if teachers gave better direction on how they should be handled, or in fact if teachers had the ability to offer better direction. What is being said here in effect is that some teachers have inadequate information skills themselves, and, inasmuch as they do not know or understand the complexity of skills within the assignment they should have some guidance on assignment preparation and the information-handling requirements relating to them. It leads to the old adage in information skills that, apart from not having the skills. you do not realize that you have information skills problems.

That would appear to justify the need for information skills instruction of teachers in schools, but I would hesitate to adduce this evidence or hypothesis to support your argument. Impugning that they have shortcomings in assignment-setting and -direction will not endear you to teachers and information skills instruction amongst them or their pupils. Much the best tactic is to find out what their information skills are, and let them 'discover' them, possibly through your illumination of the various needs for information skills teaching amongst the pupils.

User needs in college libraries

There has always been a belief that if library skills were taught effectively and regularly throughout primary and secondary school, library skills instruction in higher education would be redundant except for some brief library orientation. The conclusion must be that they are taught neither effectively nor regularly in schools because there is a continuing, substantial amount of instruction going on in higher education. What is more alarming is that those college students who are questioned on their library instruction in school often disagree that they have had any.

It is a similar story with the teaching of study skills in schools and study skills in higher education.

There are several possible reasons for this situation. First of all there is little continuity between school and college, certainly not enough for students to be able to carry enough information skills from one sector to another. The second is that there can be little continuity between school and college, because the two sectors are such different environments that it is not possible to carry more than a few information skills from one to the other. Other reasons include students' inability to recall the skills being taught, or the skills themselves, but whatever the reason there seems to be a need for a whole range of information skills teaching in colleges.

Two points are indisputable and these are that reinforcement of information skills is necessary in colleges and that the information skills have to be applied to new sets of problems.

As far as library skills are concerned then the student will not have encountered such a large (even in the small college library) collection previously, except for some acquaintance with the public library. Orientation to the library will be required therefore.

At this early stage there is also the need for those elements of information skills which are usually called study skills. The fact that there are probably lecturers who specialise in study skills teaching seems to be sufficient reason for them being taught to students. Incidentally, it is curious to be told occasionally that the reason for specific programmes of study skills instruction in colleges of higher and further education is the students are lower-ability students and therefore require more assistance with study. The implication is that high-ability students do not require instruction in study techniques!

Almost immediately after the beginning of the course further needs for information skills become apparent. This is not the case in every course but in a growing number of courses validated by TEC, BEC, SCOTEC and SCOTBEC there is a requirement that the students should acquire certain information skills. It is important to stress that this is a course *requirement* and not an expressed *need* on the part of the student. Nevertheless these course directives are based on analysis of the need of the subject, and in practical terms it is a useful 'stick' in making information skills instruction more acceptable. Many of these course requirements are only objectives and do not lay down precisely what can or should be taught. Thus the college librarian may still have the difficult task of persuading lecturers that a programme of information skills should be included in the curriculum and what its content should be.

Later in the courses, although usually not much later, more needs for information skills become apparent. As with schools and the pupils' work on assignments, so with colleges and the students' work on projects stimulates real needs. In contrast to universities and polytechnics these student projects come relatively early in the students' courses.

Finally attention should be given to the fact that in colleges a high proportion of the courses are vocational. This is a noteworthy point to be made in the context of information skills teaching. The courses take a more non-academic, practical, problem-solving approach, unlike the more academically orientated universities and polytechnics. This approach in the colleges begins early in the course and continues throughout the course and beyond, and it is a constraining and guiding discipline for the college librarian. Anything not obviously related to vocational courses and their student needs is more obviously redundant.

Yet there is one compensation for this necessity to keep to vocational requirements and that is that short-term and long-term information skills needs tend to merge in the college sector.

User needs in public libraries

Investigations of the needs for information skills training of identifiable groups using public libraries are frustrated by the problem that the diversity of possible groups is so great and even then information on the different groups is not easily available. There is no captive audience.

Mainly for this reason the programmes of information skills in public libraries are so few. Those that are put together are concerned chiefly with library skills only. The width and generality of their content is also possibly a reflection of lack of knowledge of the real needs of the users.

Programmes for specific groups should fare better. Those run for schoolchildren in association with schools, for example, should be able to focus on the information skills needs of these pupils. Some schools do provide a little information on current class work, but the information is generally inadequate. The public libraries sometimes are able to draw upon their own experience of what the pupils need, when they may be suddenly without warning descended upon by a host of earnest young searchers preparing a school assignment. Those public libraries which have staff with a direct responsibility for the school library service and are therefore closely linked to schools have the best opportunity for information on pupils' needs. They can occasionally do better than the school with a librarian, because more information work falls upon the teacher, who expresses the need to the public library.

User needs in special libraries

If we assume that the special library we have in mind is in a non-educational establishment, for example, an industrial and commercial company, or a government department, then we must try to think of information skills teaching in a rather different light.

The users' needs for information skills have to be viewed differently as well. While in schools, colleges, etc it is the individual's information skills needs, as part of his or her educational development, that are the basis for the information skills programme, in special libraries the individual's information skills needs are subsumed within the company's needs. In this case not only must the individual's objectives (as well as the programme objectives) be compatible with the organization's objectives, it is the company's objectives that dominate all other matters. This might sound extreme but it is the case that all those working within the organization are working towards its development and success — with of course the probability that if the company succeeds the employees gain as well.

But the company is a collection of people — many different kinds of managers (of whom the librarian is one), technicians, research workers, secretarial staff, etc. It is just as appropriate in this sector therefore to think in terms of user groups and their needs. The most important target group for information skills training will be the top managers.

To talk of an explicit information skills programme is, for this group however, inappropriate. Better to think along the lines of raising their information consciousness, making them aware of the importance of information (and hence information skills) for the organization. For example, lack of awareness of information which is accessible from everyday sources has cost and continues to cost many companies large and small (even government departments also) very large sums of money or advantages over competitors. Unfortunate circumstances can cause this, but lack of awareness of the importance and the lack of information retrieval skills can be a strong contributory factor. Raising this information consciousness in top management may not be as difficult as you might think. They already know the value of good, up-to-date information in decision-making.

Other, more specific information skills, like communication skills, cause information gaps, delays and misinterpretation. Lack of adequate skills in interpreting and evaluating information have the same consequence. Poor ability to organize information likewise can cause information deficiency. Thus the range of necessary information skills within the organization can be very wide.

The preliminary step is to make the top managers aware of information and its importance. Through them decisions can be taken so that the various, necessary skills are acquired by other personnel in the organization. And the argument should be that the organization needs information skills for all its staff at all levels.

Chapter Six

Programme content

Introduction

The content of an information skills programme can only be determined when, firstly, the user and his or her needs have been ascertained, and secondly, the objectives (and in particular the enabling objectives) have been settled. Perhaps by the nature of their work, librarians and information workers too often search for completeness, and this is too often reflected in their programmes of information skills. The temptation to include every conceivable information skill and instruction in every form of information source in every programme must be resisted. Consideration of the user's needs and everyone's aims and objectives may mean an apparently lop-sided programme but it will be relevant and that is the motivation the user needs in any teaching programme. Non-essentials are quickly noticed by those on the receiving end of a programme, and the result is at best forbearance of your indulgence, and at worst a general disinterest in your programme.

On the following few pages there are what might be termed 'checklists' of information skills with some discussion of the various categories. It is intended only as a source-list from which you might draw the elements your programme requires. The circumstances which would demand instruction in all of these skills would be exceptional indeed.

Traditionally the approach to designing the content of a *library* instruction programme has been to consider it as a series of levels. Most frequently in academic libraries (including college libraries) the number has been two or three (library orientation and then different levels of bibliographical instruction). In schools regular library lessons in different years have permitted many levels. In public libraries and special libraries the programme is often telescoped into one course. The variations have been extraordinarily wide and the results only moderately successful. Clearly if I put forward another prescriptive approach modelled along the traditional library instruction lines it would not be applicable to all sectors and even if it were it would be unlikely to work. Anyway the extra dimensions which are brought in by adding study skills calls for a completely different tactic. It is based on the analysis of information skills and its separation into component parts. It is also partly based on the analysis of a number of information-handling tasks.

The scope of information skills
Let me first of all make two statements:
1 The library is only one out of many information units that are concerned with information and which are sources of information.
2 Information handling has many facets, including information retrieval, information organization, information communication and information evaluation.

If you accept these statements, and they are difficult to refute, it becomes easier to understand the wide scope of information skills, and the relatively narrow scope of library skills.

Let me make a third statement:
3 The essential difference between a programme of library skills instruction and a programme of information skills instruction is that the former is library-centred and the latter is information-centred.

These three statements are presented by way of explanation and justification for what follows. You may not agree that wide-ranging information skills teaching is within your province or your capabilities, and that, as librarians, you should concern yourself only with library skills. If you do argue thus, then you should still be able to draw enough from the following pages to build a coherent programme of purely library skills. If, however, you accept the opportunity to teach information skills with this wide interpretation, then I believe you stand a good chance of success if you structure the content of your programme in the way it is outlined here.

The key is the structure. One could simply list the information skills in any sort of order. After all this is how they are often taught, and indeed how you might have to teach them. But one of the features of information skills, as they are currently interpreted, is that they are not only wide-ranging but they seem to be all-pervasive. This can cause problems.

For example, other personnel in your organization might be concerned by the possibility that some of your information skills could overlap with some of the skills they are teaching (this might be especially so in schools and colleges on the question of study skills). If you can state your information skills precisely and place them in a proper framework, then these personnel might find it easier to recognize and even put it into the context of their own work. Secondly, as far as your target audience is concerned they not only have difficulty in finding the relevance of information skills in their work, but also they have difficulty in perceiving the relationship between the different information skills.

To illustrate this structure (it is more a classification), I go back to the introduction to this book, where I suggested that study skills, communication skills, etc could be translated into terms like the organization of information, the evaluation of information, the communication of information, and the retrieval of information. These terms form the basis of this classification or ordering of information skills.

Where, you might say, have all the library skills gone? Well, the library orientation component (that is, orientation to library services) remains, but lies outside the programme. The remaining library skills are subsumed within the framework: for example, 'preparing bibliographical references' comes under 'communicating information', and 'using indexes' comes under 'retrieving information'. You might dispute the placement of some of the skills, and you would be right to do so. The complicated nature of information processes means that some skills can be interpreted in different ways and there are skills which have more than one facet: for example, memory skills, which are as much about organizing information as retrieving information.

Classification of information skills

Retrieving information
1 Search strategies
2 Reading skills

3 Sources of information
4 Using indexes
5 Using abstracts
6 Interpersonal skills
7 Listening skills
8 Keeping up-to-date with information
9 Observational skills

Evaluating information
1 Selecting information
2 Evaluating books, journal articles, etc
3 Interpreting data, original documents, etc

Organizing information
1 Note-taking from lectures
2 Note-taking from books
3 Memory skills
4 Personal indexing/personally storing the information
5 Organization of information in general

Communicating skills
1 Essay writing
2 Examination techniques
3 Report writing
4 Thesis/dissertation writing
5 Writing abstracts
6 Preparing bibliographical references
7 Writing skills

Retrieving information
Retrieving information from the library has traditionally been the core of the library skills course. That is hardly surprising because librarians are simply passing on one of their two main working functions — organizing the literature and retrieving the literature (or is it more correct to say retrieving information from the literature).

This is a major set of skills (including search strategies, using indexes, etc) and the place of these library skills is fully justified on the information skills programme. But the skills of retrieving information should not just be confined to information in the library or information unit; there are many other sources of information — animate as well as inanimate. For example, many scientists in giving information sources their order of preference often rank their research colleagues above the library — 'go to someone who knows'.

Organizing information

Traditional library skills instruction has generally been primarily concerned with how information is gathered, packaged and stored in libraries. Attention focuses on the organization of services in an individual library, and on the organization and structure of the literature held in libraries in general and in that library in particular. This is one dimension of organizing information. The other is the individual's organization of information — how he or she organizes information that has already been retrieved (for example, organizing card index files). In traditional library skills instruction this dimension usually has the lower priority, though the balance is not always a conscious decision. However, once the decision has been taken to restrict instruction to library skills a number of information-organizing skills will automatically drop out (for example, note-taking from lectures or books).

In this book the scope of information skills goes beyond the skills for one library, and beyond libraries into the wider world of information. Arguably in this situation at least as much emphasis should go on the individual's organization of information for a number of environments beyond the library, on the most effective, efficient ways for an individual to organize the information he or she has gathered, and how to organize it for re-use.

This term 're-use' and the similar term 'retrieval' are keywords here. As far as individualized information-organization skills are concerned they should be the watchwords in assessing for relevance the techniques to be taught. There are some methods of information organization which do not ensure easy re-use or retrieval of the information. This applies sometimes even to libraries where the organization of some material can make access for use more difficult for the user, and can result in user education programmes being set up to overcome their problems. However, in the small library or information unit, where some of the principles of librarianship are followed with sometimes more than a little degree of flexibility, this tends to be less the case. The fact that the fewer library personnel in these units are often continually active, as both organizers and retrievers may have something to do with this.

While you may have little difficulty in determining how much you should tell your users about the organization of the services of your library or information unit, the question of how much you should tell them about the organization of your stock in particular and the organization of the literature at large always seems to be a problem. The first part is a further case of library orientation, but the second part is a matter of how complete a picture you want to paint of the structure of the literature. The determining factors should usually be what is conveniently accessible to the user, and what the user needs − it is frustrating for the user to have described and discussed reference materials which he or she cannot have normal access to. Using this as a criterion, one can end up with some orientation and instruction which is patchy, because the small library or information unit will have very limited stock. But this is offset by a better match between information need and information instruction.

Evaluating information
This is one of the most difficult information skills to teach, and it is also one of the most sensitive areas you have to deal with.

Consider the latter problem first. Library and information personnel are normally associated with acquiring, organizing and disseminating information. That is recognized as part of their job. What is not regarded as their job is to evaluate the material that passes through their hands. Frequently, of course, the material is of such quantity that there is no time to do this; but usually it is the case that they do not have the subject expertise to put a valid opinion on the material. In some subjects like history it is not only beyond their competence but the subject itself is the interpretation and evaluation of the historical evidence and sources. It is no surprise then to find that information skills teaching in history by librarians is mainly limited to descriptions of information sources. To try to teach evaluation and interpretative skills would be regarded as an intrusion by teaching staff.

Nevertheless library and information personnel do learn (through their training) and practise (through their everyday work) evaluation skills, which they can and should (if the need arises) pass on to their users. For example, they learn how to evaluate reference books — encyclopaedias, dictionaries, atlases, etc — in terms of currency, bias, authority, etc. It is learned usually for the purpose of library stock selection, but since in this book we are looking well beyond the library environment where the user will encounter material of widely varying quality, these evaluation skills would be valuable. And the application of evaluation skills need not be limited to books and other printed materials: films, radio broadcasts, television documentaries, and even simple photographs, are all information sources carrying the same qualities and flaws as printed materials, and so arguably the skills of evaluation and interpretation are needed for them too.

Teaching the user how to evaluate printed and non-printed materials is, however, just one aspect of this skill. Equally if not more important is teaching the user when to evaluate these materials. Just as there was implicit faith in the truth of the printed word, so there is now a similar faith in the audiovisual — we readily believe the evidence of our eyes and ears. Television newsreels, for example, appear to have a truth about them because we see what seems to be happening. But subsequent analysis of some old newsreels (for example, cinema newsreels) reveals that although what you see may be true, the complete programme may be a compilation of footage from different times, from different places, and other footage may have been 'selected out'. Where politically sensitive and emotionally sensitive issues are covered (for example, war, environmental issues, etc) the evaluation skills should be brought to bear on the evidence.

Communicating information

Only rarely do you find a librarian admitting to having a communication skills component in his or her information skills programme. Yet in the majority of programmes which avowedly are concerned only with library skills, there are usually one or two skills taught which are in fact communication skills. This is hardly at all surprising because the 'entrée' or 'raison d'être' for so many library skills programmes in the educational sectors is the class assignment or project, which, apart from tutorials, seminars and examinations, is the chief method a student has of expressing himself in a careful and measured way. At least some of the skills that are taught by librarians in these circumstances are, if they are not techniques of communication, contributions to improved communication.

The list of communication skills given earlier mainly comprises techniques for the preparation of different types of document — the essay, the technical report, the dissertation, the thesis, etc — and constituent parts of some of these documents — abstracts, bibliographical references, etc. This is fair enough, but what tends to be ignored are the writing skills which are common to all documents, such as good and simple style. These are not easy skills either to teach or to acquire but if the basics of good writing are included in instruction for these different types of documents then some progress can be made to the easier transference of information skills (in particular the communication of information). Sadly, however, the different requirements of the school essay, the college essay, the college project report, the company report, and so on, make this difficult and you have to tailor your instruction to meet those needs.

Putting the content together in a programme
Your programme of information skills instruction should be, as was stressed in the last chapter, a response or a set of responses to a need for information skills. The opportunity for these responses varies from one sector to another. Two of the most common opportunities arise in schools and colleges.

In schools assignments are given to all children at all levels. Ask yourself what are the information skills that may be required to complete an assignment. As a first approximation it might be broken down into the following stages:
1 Retrieving the information
2 Evaluating the information
3 Organizing the information
4 Communicating the information
These stages may be further broken down as follows:
1 Retrieving the information — (a) Search strategies
　　　　　　　　　　　　　　　　(b) Using indexes
2 Evaluating the information — (a) Selection of information
3 Organizing the information — (a) Note-taking from books
　　　　　　　　　　　　　　　　(b) Personally storing the information

4 Communicating the infor-
   mation   — (a) Assignment writing
The skills on the right hand side would therefore form the
content of your programme of information skills when the
assignment is the task which prompts the need for information skills.

In colleges a special type of assignment is the project or
small dissertation. The procedure for determining the skills is
the same as above and basically much the same set of skills is
involved, although some of them are at a higher level. Thus
in a college when the project is the task which prompts
the need for information skills, the programme of information
skills instruction might be:

1 Retrieving the information — (a) Sources of information
                             (b) Search strategies
                             (c) Using indexes
                             (d) Using abstracts
2 Evaluating the information — (a) Selecting information
                             (b) Evaluating information
3 Organizing the information — (a) Note-taking from books,
                                 journals, etc
                             (b) Personally storing infor-
                                 mation
4 Communicating the infor- — (a) Dissertation writing
   mation   (b) Writing abstracts
                             (c) Preparing bibliographi-
                                 cal references

In special libraries similar tasks (like preparing company
reports) may provide the opportunity for strategies like the
above. In public libraries the opportunity to align a programme to a specific task is seldom possible, but a selection
from each of the main stages (retrieval, evaluation, organization and communication) could form a general programme.

Chapter Seven

Choosing teaching methods

Introduction
This chapter and the next consider the methods and the
modes of teaching information skills. These two terms,
methods and modes, are often used interchangeably, and
although it is not absolutely vital to differentiate between
them, there are advantages in so doing, primarily because it
brings a little more order into the many possible ways of
teaching.

We define 'method' as the form or procedure for teaching
information skills. Examples of teaching methods are formal
courses, course-related instruction, course-integrated instruction, and point-of-use instruction. These methods are not
mutually exclusive and it is possible to use more than one at
the same time within your programme.

We define 'mode' as the manner of doing the methods.
Examples of teaching modes are lectures, printed materials,
audiovisual presentations, and computer-assisted instruction.
For any one method, say a formal, separate course, it is
possible, usual and indeed recommended that more than one
mode is used.

There are inherent advantages and disadvantages in each of
these methods and modes, and the approach in this and the
next chapter will be to note them and then discuss the
methods and modes in the context of their application in a
small library or information unit — in schools, colleges, public
and special libraries.

As far as teaching methods are concerned, the options
vary very much from sector to sector, the choice being wide
in schools and colleges (because they are educational institutions with curricula and courses) and narrow in public

libraries and special libraries (because they are primarily non-educational establishments without curricula and courses).

In the Introduction it was emphasized that a programme of information skills 'does not [necessarily] imply a continuous, formal course of instruction, but rather a series of actions which taken together would be a consistent and coherent approach to the teaching of information skills'. Here in this chapter we are at last deciding the form and shape that this programme should take.

Formal courses

The formal course is a course which is complete on its own, without reference to any other course. It usually comprises a series of lectures with exercises and assignments, but it can include any number and variety of teaching modes, and the length is entirely flexible.

This option should read 'formal, separate courses' or, if we are dealing with schools and colleges, 'formal courses outside the curriculum'. It denotes completeness and finiteness. It has a beginning, a middle and an end, it is compact and it is coherent. From this point of view the formal course is easier to plan and organize than other methods. But 'separate' and 'outside' also imply detachment and isolation, and in the case of schools and colleges this means separation from other educational programmes.

Many have argued that information skills are of such importance that they merit a separate, formal course of their own — a GCE in Information Skills if you like. There is then a danger that it becomes more like an academic discipline than a set of skills or techniques. And there is a further danger (and this occurs especially with courses concerned solely with library skills) that the course tends to become more appropriate to the training of professional librarians rather than the training of ordinary users of information sources.

The above comments are general points for and against teaching information skills through a formal course. Further advantages and disadvantages are noted as follows, but remember that courses can vary in as many ways as you want (length, content, teaching modes, etc) and not all may necessarily apply to every situation.

Advantages	*Disadvantages*
1 Permits a wide range of information to be taught	1 Difficult to maintain relevance and interest throughout the course
2 The contents of the programme are readily seen as a coherent whole	2 Unless 'credits' or some such inducements are offered as part of the course, it is difficult to inspire and maintain motivation
3 Very flexible in its ability to use any number of teaching modes	3 Requires a high degree of commitment and time to planning and execution
	4 Probably needs the organization's approval before setting it up
	5 Can be difficult to schedule into the user's time
	6 The course could be competing with other (academic) courses

The formal course sounds and generally is a large undertaking, and is often beyond the resources of the small library and information unit of a school or a college.

In public libraries, however, many of their programmes of information skills are formal courses. They tend to concentrate on library skills and library operations, and barely touch upon other information skills, unless they are programmed as part of an adult education series. You can expect all the disadvantages noted above, and also, it has to be said, small initial numbers accompanied by discouraging dropping out of course participants.

Unfortunately in the public library sector (and it can be the same in the special library sector) you may have little choice, unless you are dealing with school groups, or an associated adult education programme. In fact this latter type of programme, in common with such curriculum courses as 'methods of social sciences information skills', means that you have more time to prepare the correct response. instruction which is considered after the next method —

course-related instruction — which is part of the step towards course-integrated instruction.

Course-related instruction

While it is always intended that a formal course of information skills should be relevant and related to other activities in the organization (for example, the students' curriculum in college) its structure and compactness can mean that it is remote. The solution is to break down this formal course into a number of component parts, each covering one or more skills, and spread them out through the year. In schools and colleges this would mean matching each part of your course to the particular needs of the curriculum at any one time. It could mean that some parts of your course would remain in your programme but others would have to be excluded. In other words the integrity of the formal course of information skills is sacrificed for the relevance of individual information skills to the needs of the curriculum. Not a bad sacrifice.

Advantages	*Disadvantages*
1 All the information skills are relevant to the course	1 It may not always be possible to schedule your instruction to the needs of the course (for example, if you are associated with several courses, demand may come from all at the same time and you do not have the resources and time to spread yourself to all)
2 The information skills programme supports and is seen to support the course	
3 Able to meet student needs at the appropriate time	
4 Flexibility, in that there is not the necessity for the sort of long-range planning required in a formal course	

Course-related instruction is usually associated with schools and colleges, yet it is just as applicable in the public library and special library sectors, if any appropriate courses are currently running in the organization. But in whatever sector you are the great need is that you have an intimate knowledge of the course and close cooperation with its teachers. Opportunities for information skills instruction may be irregular, but good anticipation of the opportunities means that you have more time to prepare the correct response.

For most educational organizations course-related instruction is the most common teaching method.

It is certainly the easiest first approach to instruction, and in a small library with limited resources of time you can approach instruction tentatively and without the danger of biting off more than you can chew, as might be the case with a formal course. It is a test-bed for the greater commitment of time and resources which is involved in course-integrated instruction, and in fact it should be seen as the first step towards the ideal of course-integrated instruction.

Course-integrated instruction

Course-integrated instruction is a further stage along the course-related/course-integrated instruction continuum. Not only is your instruction associated with the course, it is now an integral part of the course. And while course-related instruction is usually fragmented, there is the possibility that a complete course unit can be planned in course-integrated instruction (just like a formal course).

Course-integrated instruction has many advantages over separate courses and course-related instruction but it carries with it many responsibilities. While in the latter methods you might be able to fudge issues like aims and objectives, here you are bound by the same objectives as the course with which you are integrated. It also carries a long-term commitment, although for those who have struggled for several years to get course-integrated instruction, this is exactly what has been pursued.

Advantages

1 All the information skills are an integral part of the course
2 All the information skills are relevant to the course
3 Able to meet student needs at the appropriate time
4 You have the support of teaching members of the course
5 It implies a long-term commitment to the teaching of information skills on the part of the organization

Disadvantages

1 Requires a high degree of commitment and time to planning and execution
2 You are only partly in control of the instruction
3 Needs the organization's approval and support before setting it up

Course-integrated instruction in schools and colleges is regarded as the ultimate achievement in information skills programme planning. Not only is your commitment to the course as full as it can be, the course's commitment to information skills is undeniable and assured. Some regard course-integrated instruction not only as desirable but essential. In truth there are some aspects of information skills (some study skills in schools, for example) which cannot sensibly be taught unless through the curriculum; that is, as an integral part of the curriculum. But if you are in the school do remember that the issue of whether information skills should be taught as part of the curriculum, or offered as such modules in every college. The modules have been hard-won, and it is up to you not to waste these initiatives. consistent within any one school — study skills may be course-integrated while library skills may be only course-related.

In colleges the possibilities for course-integrated instruction are highest of all. National validating bodies like TEC and BEC sanction and support the inclusion of information skills units or modules in some of their courses. The amount and depth varies from subject to subject, and you still have to negotiate with your college and its lecturers on the exact nature of the units. The responsibility for the teaching of these information skills may not be yours or you may have to share the work with study skills specialists, but the opportunities for involvement are there. These nationally-validated courses, are, with the exception of a few CNAA-validated library skills units, unique. But there is one further responsibility incumbent upon you — your particular effort and its success or failure can influence the long-term prospects of such modules in every college. They have been hard-won, and it is up to you not to waste these initiatives.

The opportunities for course-integrated information skills instruction in public and special libraries are few if any, because they are not 'per se' educational organizations. Yet public libraries do have in part the function to educate and they are often associated with educational programmes; and special libraries can be of many sorts, belonging to a variety of organizations including those which are primarily educational.

The public library's association with courses of adult education and adult literacy are two examples where the chances of course-integrated instruction are high. This is because local authorities have ultimate responsibility for most educational enterprises within their region, as well as the public library service. In the case of adult literacy programmes elements of information skills would seem to be an obvious component of such programmes.

Point-of-use instruction

Finally, there are the self-instructional methods, where the emphasis is switched to the information user learning rather than being taught. Point-of-use instruction is the most widely-known self-instructional method, but examples of its use are hard to come by and it is the least-used of all teaching methods. It means instruction that is available at the point of use and at the point of need, and it is normally associated with learning how to use special reference material in libraries.

Several different modes of instruction are possible with this method, but usually they are either printed materials (instructional sheets or posters) or audiovisual presentations (audio-tapes, videotapes or tape-slides). As we shall see later, each of these modes has advantages and disadvantages, and reference should be made to these also. Here we simply note the general advantages and disadvantages of the teaching method.

Advantages
1 Constantly available to the user
2 Uniformity of presentation
3 Can be re-read or replayed for reinforcement and for difficult points
4 Inexpensive (if printed matter used)
5 Available at the point of need
6 Available at the time of need
7 Can be self-pacing

Disadvantages
1 A degree of motivation for use is required of the user
2 Effectiveness difficult to evaluate
3 Expensive (if audiovisual presentations used)
4 Security is a problem if audiovisual presentations used
5 May be difficult to find space for it

Point-of-use instruction has always promised so much in library skills instruction because it is instruction that is available when and where it is needed. But it never seems to have been really successful, either because the instructional point and the instructional material at that point are overlooked by the library user or the instructional material is poorly presented.

To the librarian in the small library or information unit it could offer a time-saving method of library orientation, library instruction and especially bibliographical instruction — but every effort has to be made to alert the user to its existence. It is of course a method which is only relevant to the library skills element of information skills. It is usable in any sector, and if well-prepared and well-publicized could lighten your teaching load, freeing you for other elements of information skills teaching.

Chapter Eight

Choosing teaching modes

Introduction
Just about every conceivable teaching mode has been used in the teaching of information skills, so there is quite a range to choose from. No attempt is made here to recommend one mode over any other, partly because the success of the various modes depends very much on the aptitude of the teacher, and partly because there is no conclusive and consistent evidence that one teaching mode is intrinsically superior to any other (and this holds good in education generally, not just in information skills teaching).

In practice, your choice will be determined by several factors:
1 Your ability to handle the teaching mode confidently
2 The financial cost of the teaching mode
3 The time required in preparing the material for a particular teaching mode
4 The likely receptivity of that teaching mode amongst your users

However, even within these limitations you still have a choice, and to make that choice this chapter enumerates the advantages and disadvantages of the various teaching modes. In two later chapters two particular groups of teaching modes (audiovisual media and printed guides) will be discussed on a slightly different dimension with a number of examples.

But before the enumeration of the advantages and disadvantages of the different teaching modes it is opportune to discuss briefly the question of group and individualized instruction.

Group and individualized instruction
Most of the teaching modes can be categorized as being
group modes or individualized modes of instruction (ie individuals can learn on their own), and a few can be labelled
as both. Thus we have

Group instruction
Lectures
Seminars
Demonstrations
Tutorials
Games or simulations

Group and individualized instruction
Tape-slides
Films
Videotapes
Audiotapes
Slides/transparencies

Individualized instruction
Books
Printed guides
Practical exercises
Programmed instruction
Self-instructional materials
Computer-assisted instruction

In practice many teachers of information skills select from
each group for their programme. This is partly because certain
instructional methods are better suited to some of their
programme content than others, partly because they recognize
that some of their students may be more susceptible to one
mode rather than another (or at least some of the students
might be motivated by one rather than another), partly out
of a desire for variety, and partly (and most importantly)
they recognize that most information skills are techniques
which can be acquired less easily through group-teaching
modes than by individualized instruction means, that is,
learning by doing. Remember that information skills are
concerned mainly with techniques, rather than abstract and
theoretical concepts.

Many teachers use in fact several teaching modes almost
simultaneously — with great effect. For example, a one-hour

session might comprise twenty minutes of formal lecture, a ten-minute audiovisual presentation, a ten-minute practical exercise, a ten-minute discussion, then a final ten minutes of lecture. The advantages of this approach are many, including:

1 The one-hour session is broken up to give variety
2 There is a proportion of learning-by-doing as well as formal lecturing
3 Some teaching modes can re-present and reinforce ideas put forward in others.

If possible try to use a mixed but balanced approach along the lines of the above. Even the disadvantages of some of the modes that are described in the following pages can be modified or reduced if used in close conjunction with other teaching modes.

Lectures

The lecture is the most traditional mode of teaching and it forms the basis of most information skills teaching. Its endurance stems largely from its use throughout education, but also because it is a very flexible mode which allows and often demands the incorporation of other teaching modes. The following advantages and disadvantages relate to the lecture in its 'pure' form.

Advantages	*Disadvantages*
1 A common, therefore familiar, mode	1 It is a one-way communication process
2 Alterations and updating are easy	2 Group-teaching method only
3 It has the flexibility to incorporate other teaching modes	3 Does not allow for different levels of ability amongst its recipients
4 It can be used in any environment — library, classroom, etc	4 The attention span of the recipients can be of very short duration (eg there is evidence to show that about ten minutes after a lecture has begun attention begins to drop significantly)
5 Inexpensive in terms of material	5 Can be rather formal

Videotapes

The use of videotapes in information skills teaching is quite small, although there is an increasing amount of information skills material produced in this format.

It is potentially a very effective teaching mode (witness its place in the Open University courses, and, of course, the power of television as a communication medium), but the advantage of its widespread availability and receptivity is much reduced unless the presentation is of the highest technical and artistic quality. In the latter terms everyday television is mostly excellent, and anything less than this standard in your presentation will distract from the content.

Advantages	*Disadvantages*
1 The medium is familiar to the user	1 Alterations and updating are difficult
2 Both group and individual teaching is possible	2 It is a one-way communication process
3 Constantly available to the user	3 Cost of materials and equipment is high
4 Can be replayed for reinforcement and for difficult points	4 Production requires a high level of expertise and much time to prepare
5 Uniformity of presentation	5 Impersonal (ie non-interactive)
6 Can portray movement	6 Does not allow for different levels of ability amongst its users
7 Can dramatize problem-solving situations	7 Subject to mechanical failure
8 Can be used in any environment — library, classroom, etc	

Tape-slides

Of all the audiovisual modes used in information skills teaching, the tape-slide is the most common. To a large extent the responsibility for this lies with libraries in the university and polytechnic sectors who have in the past formed groups to produce programmes. There is also a substantial number of commercially-produced tape-slides.

Since both commercial and non-commercial productions are geared towards the university and polytechnic market, their value to the small library and information unit is small.

Advantages	*Disadvantages*
1 Both group and individual teaching is possible	1 The medium is unfamiliar to the user
2 Constantly available to the user	2 It is a one-way communication process
3 Can be replayed for reinforcement and for difficult points	3 Alterations and updating are difficult
4 Uniformity of presentation	4 Production requires a high level of expertise and much time to prepare
5 Can dramatize problem-solving situations	5 Impersonal (ie non-interactive)
6 Can be used in any environment — library, classroom, etc	6 Does not allow for different levels of ability amongst its users
7 Cost of materials and equipment is relatively low	7 Subject to mechanical failure

Audiotapes

It is surprising that the audiotape or the audiocassette tape is not used more frequently in information skills instruction, because it has many advantages, while some of its disadvantages can easily be countered if used self-instructionally in tandem with practical exercises and teaching handouts: it is an ideal tool in the point-of-use method of instruction. Yet all too often it is hidden away in some small corner and hardly publicized, so the user is either not aware of it or has to use some initiative to get it.

Advantages	*Disadvantages*
1 The medium is familiar to the user	1 It is a one-way communication process
2 Both group and individual teaching possible	2 Impersonal, ie non-interactive
3 Constantly available to the user	3 Does not allow for different levels of ability amongst its users
4 Can be replayed for reinforcement and for difficult points	4 Subject to mechanical failure
5 Uniformity of presentation	5 Can be a security problem if it is left at point-of-use
6 Can dramatize problem-solving situations	

Advantages

7 Can be used in any environment — library, classroom, etc
8 Cost of materials and equipment relatively low
9 Production does not
   require great expertise
   and much time to prepare
10 Can be self-pacing
11 Can be made available at
   the point-of-use
12 Alterations and updating
   are not difficult

Computer-assisted instruction

Some discussion on the use of computer-assisted instruction
as a teaching mode is included here, not just for the sake of
completeness nor as a nod to the future, but because even in
the most unpromising, small organization, there may be
possibilities of using it. In the notes that follow it is the
microcomputer that is considered: the use of main-frame
computers has rarely been a viable option for information
skills teaching even in the largest library.

Only a few years ago you would not have expected the
microcomputer to make an imminent appearance in almost
every secondary school in the UK, yet microcomputer-
assisted instruction has now become a feasible mode of
instruction for information skills there. The software on
information-handling skills is still in short supply, although
it is being produced in some quantity in the USA.

The microcomputer was drafted into schools purely for
educational purposes, not administrative functions. It is
possible that the microcomputer could be brought into your
library or information unit for the same reason, but more
likely (in the colleges and special libraries sectors) it would
be brought in to assist in organizational procedures. But once
you have them they can change their function!

Advantages	*Disadvantages*
1 Constantly available to the user	1 Alterations and updating are difficult

Advantages	*Disadvantages*
2 Can be replayed for re-inforcement and for difficult points	2 Cost of materials and equipment is high
3 Can be self-pacing	3 Production of software requires a high level of expertise and much time to prepare
4 Information on learning progress could be available to the user	4 Subject to mechanical failure
5 Uniformity of presentation	5 Users need to be trained to use the equipment
6 Can be interactive	
7 Can allow for different levels of ability amongst its users	

Chapter Nine

Audiovisual presentations

Introduction

In the chapter on teaching modes the advantages and disadvantages of three particular audiovisual modes (videotapes, tape-slides, and audiotapes) were noted. The intention here is not to repeat the arguments but to consider the use made of the modes in the context of the small library or information unit, and to list a number of presentations that could be used by the small unit.

The choice of the term 'audiovisual presentations' instead of 'audiovisual modes' was deliberate. You don't have to see many audiovisual presentations before you come to the conclusion that, rightly or wrongly, there is a noticeable attempt at entertainment, artistry, if not drama in them, whether it is in the camera shots or the music. This does not necessarily obscure the teaching in them, and in fact it can give the presentation more impact. The audiovisual presentation is somewhat different from other teaching modes, and can be used as a counterbalance to more formal teaching modes. And they are also different in that they tend to be harshly criticized when reviewed, possibly because they invite comparison with our daily television diet. Remember then that your target groups probably watch television too.

In-house production

Very few school, college, public or special libraries produce audiovisual presentations, and the obvious reasons are lack of money, lack of time and lack of expertise. Your unit will almost certainly be in the same position.

Although an audiotape is cheap in terms of materials, technically it is deceptively difficult to produce one with good sound quality. A tape-slide looks cheap and easy — a couple of reels of film and a cassette tape and you are on your way, but £500 is a relatively small sum to lay out if it is properly costed in terms of both materials and labour. Technically and artistically it is by no means a simple task, and there are many poor presentations to testify to this. When it comes to videotape and film the production costs really escalate because you are almost entirely reliant on the professional. Think in terms of £2000-£4000 and you won't be far out in your estimates.

But even if your parent organization has the resources and inclination to make a presentation for you (with or without your assistance), you ought to consider the morality of agreeing to the expenditure if it is a significant proportion of your annual budget for stock and staff.

Buying, hiring and borrowing and the pros and cons of audio-visual media

You may be able to buy, hire or borrow audiovisual presentations produced elsewhere, but you have to choose carefully and wisely.

Obviously you will select presentations which are appropriate and relevant to your type of library or information unit, and the level of those to be taught; ie in a college library you will generally choose something that has been produced by or for a college library. However, you have to be a little more circumspect than this: the college library which screened a tape-slide which featured instruction in the use of *Science citation index* (albeit only a small part), when the library neither subscribed to it nor had any prospect of a subscription, is perhaps not exceptional. In a small library or information unit the probability of this happening is high, and if it does it can simply tantalize and frustrate your users.

But apart from the problem of not having the relevant stock featured in the presentations, you may find that valuable time is taken up in having to modify other parts of the information skills programme to incorporate such outside support. You are unlikely to be able to alter these presentations so your own teaching must be modified to accommodate them in your programme neatly. Be wary of allowing the audio-visual presentations to dominate your programme and its content. Very few coherent information skills programmes have been built entirely around a suite of audiovisual presentations.

Audiovisual media can be an advantage if there are large numbers of participants in your programme. With group viewing, you can save yourself time and also much wear and tear caused by repetition of the same teaching. And if you recommend the presentations be used in a self-instructional mode, then the participants can get on with it themselves, thus saving you further time.

But one of your trump cards in your size of information unit is, we hope, your close, personal contact with your users — not forgetting the argument that the optimum situation for teaching information skills is the one-to-one dialogue. Should you throw away this asset of close contact and good rapport with the user, in favour of what can be a somewhat impersonal set of teaching modes? Of course not. By all means make moderate use of audiovisual media but don't let it isolate you from the user.

What is available?
Having weighed the pros and cons of audiovisual media and decided in favour of them, what is available to you? Unfortunately not a tremendous amount that would be appropriate to you in the small library or information unit — and tracking down the suitable media is not easy either.

The large, national and general catalogues and bibliographies of audiovisual material are of little assistance here. You need to refer to the regularly-updated, specialist, information skills catalogue produced by the British Library Information Officer for User Education Project at Loughborough University of Technology.[1] Although not critically annotated it does offer full bibliographical details and descriptive summaries of relevant media, and information on their hire and purchase. Many are not entirely suitable for small libraries and information units, so the following lists are given as a careful selection of the most appropriate items, which could be used and are currently available.

They can be grouped as follows:

1 Promotional guides to libraries and information services
2 Guides to information techniques
3 Guides to forms of literature

4 Guides to single, specific information sources or services
5 Guides to the subject literature by discipline

Besides the brief, descriptive details, there are short, indicative summaries of content, and of their possible applicability for the four sectors of schools, colleges, public libraries and special libraries.

1 Promotional guides to libraries and information services
Obviously there will be no presentation which introduces your particular service, but there may be one which promotes your type of service, for example, the public library. These promotional presentations can be valuable as 'ice-breakers' at the beginning of a programme of information skills. The best of them paint a broad picture of libraries in the context of total information resources, and illustrate the relationship of one type of library or information service to other similar services. They should not attempt to instruct but simply promote; if they do no more than instil a good 'attitude' to libraries and information services, then they are doing well. Unfortunately, with the possible exception of the first one noted, there are none which just try to promote the concept and idea of information in its broadest sense. There are, however, many presentations here and elsewhere in these lists which do open in this way.

1 *Information retrieval: Why?* (Roy J Adams)
   Tape-slide, 7½ minutes, 36 slides, colour
      Discusses the need for information in modern society for business and industry. It shows how the process of information transfer works and briefly shows one of the major types of information tools: abstracting and indexing services. The programme concentrates on the 'Why?' of information retrieval.
   (Suitable for TEC and BEC students in colleges)

2 *Where do I start?* (PAVIC Publications)
   Videocassette, 7 minutes, colour
      Introduces students to the library, explaining the arrangement of stock, highlights the various services. It is not intended to give detailed instruction on a specific library or particular service, but to give general information on and promote positive attitudes towards libraries in higher education.

(Suitable for new students in institutions of further and higher education).

3 *Desk-bound* (London Business School)
Tape-slide, 15 minutes, black & white
> Aims to persuade people to make use of the library first before proceeding to gather new data. It does not aim to teach the details of the stock of any particular library, or what are the best sources on any specific topic. It attempts to prompt individuals to their information needs, and to find out which information sources can meet them.

(Suitable for students in institutions of further and higher education preparing a project)

4 *Books and libraries* (Open University Educational Enterprises Ltd)
Film or videocassette, 24 minutes, colour.
> Concerned with the philosophy and attitudes of the public library system, and describes the service· of a typical public library.

(Suitable for public libraries)

5 *Using libraries: the public library* (Open University Educational Enterprises Ltd)
Film or videocassette, 24 minutes, colour
> Although focusing on a particular library, it could be used to show the scope and services of public libraries generally.

(Suitable for public libraries)

6 *Introducing books* (Educational Video Index)
Videocassette, 20 minutes, colour
> An illustration of the way a school librarian can co-operate with a classteacher to introduce a variety of books to his/her class, and the classwork that can develop from the scheme. The programme was recorded with a mixed-ability class of twelve-year olds.

(Suitable for schools)

2 Guides to information techniques

There is no lack of material in this section. This is partly a reflection of the wide range of information skills as we interpret them. They have been produced by an equally wide range of publishers, mostly from outside the library and information world. This means that in most cases the library is not featured or even mentioned.

In spite of the supposed universality of some information skills, most of the presentations are geared to particular sectors, but with discrimination some can be used in several sectors.

1 *Study patterns No 4: Note-taking* (University of Strathclyde, Centre for Educational Practice)
  Videocassette, 19 minutes, black & white
   The programme centres on the presentation of a standard passage about the advantages of television in education. The presenter shows different methods of taking notes from the spoken passage, and illustrates principles of summarizing and organizing significant ideas, and this is followed by some basic hints in the use of notes.
  (Suitable for students in colleges, and even sixth-formers)

2 *Study patterns No 5: Essay-writing* (University of Strathclyde, Centre for Educational Practice)
  Videocassette, 17 minutes, black & white
   This is organized around the writing of a real essay on a literary theme, and shows all stages from the original sketch-ideas to the final product. The material shown is unedited from the drafts used by the writer of the essay shown. Basic principles of selection of material, organization of ideas, drafting, correcting and final presentation are incorporated.
  (Suitable for students in colleges, and even sixth-formers)

3 *Making numbers work* (Melrose Film Productions)
  Videocassette, 25 minutes, colour
   Designed to improve the presentation and increase the usefulness of numerical data. Deals with the best presentation of statistical data (drastic rounding, verbal summaries, etc), effective presentation of graphs, and so on.
  (Suitable for special libraries)

4 *Listen!* (Melrose Film Productions)
  Videocassette, 19 minutes, colour
   Deals with listening skills — how to listen effectively, how to communicate through listening, and so on.
  (Suitable for special libraries primarily, but other sectors as well, apart from schools)

5 *The writing programme* (Melrose Film Productions)
 Videocassette, 19 minutes, colour
   Suggests five simple rules (and one question) which help
   people to write more clearly and present their writing
   more helpfully.
 (Suitable for all sectors except schools)

6 *Effective learning: a practical guide for students* (Tetradon
 Publications)
 Audiotape
   Comprises a number of exercises, including preparing
   good lecture notes, finding out about the library, get-
   ting the most out of a book, and using resource materials.
 (Suitable for new students about to start college)

7 *Using books* (Newcastle upon Tyne Polytechnic Products
 Ltd)
 Tape-slide, 10½ minutes, 55 slides, colour
   Discusses various methods of evaluating books, such as
   examining contents pages and indexes in order to
   give students some advice on choosing books suitable to
   their needs and purposes.

8 *Access skills* (Concord Films Council Ltd)
 Videocassette, 10 minutes, black & whiᵗ
   Part of an adult learning and basic skills unit, it shows
   some activities that can be used to develop the skills
   needed to locate information.
 (Suitable for public libraries)

9 *Listening and note-taking* (Evans Brothers Ltd)
 2 audiocassettes
   The programme is intended for those who need to
   listen to talks and retain a large proportion of what is
   said. It comprises three parts: exercises in immediate
   recall, outline writing, and practice in simultaneous
   note-taking.
 (Suitable for schoolchildren but could be used with
 students in the higher age groups)

10 *How to study* (Encyclopaedia Britannica International Ltd)
 Audiocassette
   Deals with a variety of study skills.
 (Suitable for schoolchildren in the higher age groups)

11 *On-line searching* (Drake Educational Associates)
    Tape-slide, 12 minutes, 76 slides, colour
    The programme is designed to provide a general intro-
    duction to on-line searching. It shows the various
    stages involved from the initial request for information
    to the final acquisition of documents. A search for
    information on the use of audio-visual aids for the
    teaching of physics is carried out on the System
    Development Corporation Orbit service. At the appro-
    priate points during the search, aspects such as the
    factors affecting the choice of a system to search on
    and the steps involved in carrying out a search, are
    discussed. The programme concludes by outlining some
    of the advantages of on-line searching.
    (Suitable for use in special libraries)

12 *Computerized information retrieval* (HERTIS Publi-
    cations)
    Videocassette, 13 minutes, colour
    Intended to provide a general introduction to the
    concept of on-line searching. Most of the programme is
    a recording of a search for references on the topic of
    video games, using the INSPEC file of Lockheed
    Dialog. The main searching techniques (and/or, trunc-
    ation, word adjacency) are shown briefly, but only to
    illustrate the potential of on-line, not to serve as full
    instructions for anyone doing a search.
    (Suitable for use in special libraries)

13 *Graffiti on a database: a lighthearted look at database
    searching* (Learned Information (Europe) Ltd)
    Tape-slide, 65 slides, colour
    Introduces the concepts and procedures of database
    searching to students and other first-time users. Struc-
    tured like a soap opera complete with a sponsor,
    advertising and music, the dramatic story line shows
    Susie Student who is inspired in her choice of a project
    topic by seeing a graffiti artist. She becomes over-
    whelmed by the volume of printed material and the
    variety of indexing and abstracting tools but is rescued
    by a librarian who tells her about computer-searchable
    bibliographic databases. The programme shows the
    advantages of computer-searching and discusses in

non-technical terms the use of boolean logic and selection of subject terms.
(Suitable for use in special libraries)

Finally in this section there are five very useful radio and television presentations, which, although not at present commercially available, are accessible in a number of school and college libraries. They are mainly suitable for school-children.

14 *Study skills* (BBC Radio)
A series of ten programmes to help students in the 14-16 age group to use information resources, organize work effectively, study for examinations, etc.

15 *Use your head* (BBC Television)
A series of ten programmes useful to teachers working with students in the 16-19 age group. It includes the skills of memory skills and reading skills. The BBC published a book based on the series by Tony Buzan in 1974.

16 *Communicate* (BBC Television)
A series which is aimed at the 14-16+ age group. It includes topics like detecting bias, interpreting graphics, and note-taking.

17 *Read on* (BBC Television)
A series of ten programmes concerned with reading skills for children in the 10-14 age group. It includes a wide range of study skills and reference skills as well as reading skills.

18 *Inside pages* (BBC Television)
A series about books (fiction and non-fiction) aimed at the 10-12 age group. Its purpose is to stimulate children to read widely and make greater use of libraries.

3 Guides to forms of literature

I hesitate to include guides to forms of literature because library and information personnel already have too great a preoccupation with breaking down information and the literature in which it is found, into sometimes quite arbitrary forms or categories. We are often more concerned with the package rather than the contents.

The library and information user does not normally approach you with a request for an encyclopaedia on microcomputers, a dictionary on microcomputers, a periodical on microcomputers, conference proceedings on microcomputers, etc. He or she simply wants a book or information on microcomputers.

Nevertheless, one must be realistic and face the fact that most libraries and information units are organized by form, and some of the forms are especially difficult to access and use.

1 *Patents today* (Newcastle upon Tyne Polytechnic Products Ltd)
Videocassette, 16 minutes, colour
   Shows the importance of patent information to industry. This is done by way of interviews with people in industry, including a director of research, a patent officer and an information officer, who all use patent information in the course of their work.
(Suitable for special libraries)

2 *Patents online* (Newcastle upon Tyne Polytechnic Products Ltd)
Videocassette, 10 minutes, colour
   Gives a brief description of how on-line searching for patents was developed, and looks at the advantages that online searching has over conventional searching techniques.
(Suitable for special libraries)

3 *Patents at work* (Newcastle upon Tyne Polytechnic Products Ltd)
Tape-slide, 12 minutes, colour
   Illustrates how patent information can be used in a rather unusual way. The story, which is based on fact, shows how patent literature was used to find information about a company to which an application for employment had been made.
(Suitable for special libraries)

4 *How to use reference books* (Bumpus, Haldane and Maxwell Ltd)
Tape-slide, 13 minutes, colour

Intended as an introductory guide to the main reference books to be found in libraries. It is arranged in two parts: part 1 is concerned with facts and figures, part 2 is concerned with people and places.

(Suitable for college libraries, public libraries and sixth-form schoolchildren)

4 *Guides to single, specific information sources or services*

As you might imagine it is the large, expensive sources and services that usually comprise this group — the juggernauts like *Science citation index*, *Chemical abstracts*, and so on. These are just the sort of information sources and services that the small library or information unit will not have. Fortunately the everyday, modest encyclopaedia is seldom so complex that it demands a sophisticated audiovisual presentation to describe it.

1 *The answer's in the abstract* (Argus Film Library Ltd)
   Film, 16 minutes
   Explains the use, and the usefulness, of abstracts in helping the busy manager to cope with management literature, illustrating this with brief studies on how Anbar Management Publications provides subscribers with the answers to their current awareness and information retrieval problems.

(Primarily suitable for the special library having Anbar Management Publications, but could also be used by any other library holding these publications)

2 *The 'Dialog' information service — worldwide information on command* (Dialog Information Services)
   Film or videocassette, 20 minutes, colour
   Beginning with a history of the Dialog service, it continues with a guided tour of the Dialog facilities, and reviews the full range of support services available through Dialog. Two sample searches are illustrated.

(Suitable for special libraries)

3 *This is Ceefax* (BBC Enterprises Ltd)
   Film or videocassette, 20 minutes, colour
   Describes how Ceefax operates, tracing its development at Kingswood Warren to the newsroom at the Television Centre where material is edited for broadcasting.

(Suitable for all Ceefax users, but especially public libraries)

5 *Guides to the subject literature by discipline*

Although there is prolific production of guides to the subject
literature, no list is given here. Almost all those available
have been produced either by libraries in universities and
polytechnics, or by commercial publishers aiming them at
these sectors. Some colleges and special libraries might find
that even those on the relevant subject have a level and orientation in the presentation that is too much geared to academic
teaching.

Publishers and distributors of audiovisual media

1 Roy J Adams
   72 Bateman Road
   East Leake
   Nr Loughborough, Leics

2 Argus Film Library Ltd
   15 Beaconsfield Road
   London NW10 2LE

3 BBC Enterprises Ltd
   54-58 Uxbridge Road
   Ealing
   London W5 2TF

4 Bumpus, Haldane and
     Maxwell Ltd
   Special Services Dept
   Olney, Bucks M46 4BN

5 Concord Films Council Ltd
   201 Felixstowe Road
   Ipswich
   Suffolk

6 Dialog Information
     Services
   Dept 40
   3460 Hillview Avenue
   Palo Alto, CA 94304, USA

7 Drake Educational
     Associates
   212 Whitchurch Road
   Cardiff CF4 3XF

8 Educational Video Index
   25 Thurloe Street
   London NW1 4SA

9 Encyclopaedia Britannica
     International Ltd
   Mappin House
   156-162 Oxford Street
   London W1N 0HJ

10 Evans Brothers Ltd
   Montague House
   Russell Square
   London WC1B 5BX

11 HERTIS Publications
   Hatfield Polytechnic
   PO Box 110
   Hatfied
   Herts AL10 9AD

12 Learned Information
     (Europe) Ltd
   Besselsleigh Road
   Abingdon
   Oxford OX13 6LG

13 London Business School
Sussex Place
Regent's Park
London NW1 4SA

14 Melrose Film Productions
8-12 Old Queen Street
London SW1H 9HP

15 Newcastle upon Tyne Poly-
technic Products Ltd
Ellison Building
Ellison Place
Newcastle upon Tyne
NE1 8ST

16 Open University Edu-
cational Enterprises
12 Cofferidge Close
Stony Stratford
Milton Keynes
MK11 1BY

17 PAVIC Publications
Department of Edu-
cation Studies
Sheffield City Polytechnic
35 Collegiate Crescent
Sheffield S10 2BP

18 University of Strathclyde
Centre for Educational
Practice
Room 6.01
Alexander Turnbull
Building
155 George Street
Glasgow

19 Tetradon Publications
40 Hadzor Road
Oldbury, Warley
West Midlands B68 9LA

Using audiovisual media
Most audiovisual presentations have been produced to make
them suitable both for group use and individualized use. When
individuals use them independently they can use them when
they want to and how they want to, they can switch them on
and off as they wish, they can use them in part or as a whole;
that is, they have complete flexibility in their use. It is no
bad thing to allow such flexibility in a formal, group teaching
session. It is not always essential or appropriate for that
matter to use the presentation in its entirety with a group,
and in fact it may become a better teaching tool if it is shown
only in part.
This flexible use of the audiovisual presentation permits
its ready integration with other teaching modes and content
in a programme of information skills. This is important,
because although most audiovisual presentations are prepared
as complete units and can therefore be used as substantive

units, they can valuably reinforce, or be reinforced by, other parts of the information skills programme. Remember also that some learners respond better to some teaching modes than to others, and therefore the presentation is an alternative approach to the same skills taught in another way elsewhere in the programme. Basically, however, the audiovisual presentation should be regarded as a teaching mode with programme content, complementary and supplementary to other parts of the programme.

Many audiovisual presentations have their own teaching notes and supplementary material available with them. Where they haven't, librarians have often prepared their own supplementary handouts. These have often been exercises or some such practical work, which reinforce, illustrate, or elaborate upon aspects of the presentation.

Reference

1 Malley, I *A catalogue of audiovisual media for the teaching of information skills.* Loughborough, INFUSE Publications, 1984.

Chapter Ten

Printed guides to information

In spite of sometimes considerable misgivings about the value
and effectiveness of printed guides in teaching information
skills, many libraries and information units regard them as a
basic part of their programme. The guides fall into four main
categories:
1 Guides to the library or information service
2 Guides to the subject literature (eg sources of information
  in textile design)
3 Guides to specific reference materials (eg a guide to the
  use of *Biological abstracts*)
4 Guides to information techniques (eg search strategies,
  writing project reports, evaluating a book)
  Large organizations like university and polytechnic
libraries invariably produce guides in all four categories,
perhaps as many as twenty in one year. Productivity is a
measure of the manpower, time and other resources a service
may have at its disposal, and consequently the smaller library
or information unit will produce few if any in a year. For this
reason it is only sensible that if you *are* going to get involved
in this sort of work, then you should ensure that your effort
is well-directed.

This chapter is intended to encourage you to think before
you put pen to paper and to ask at least some of the right
questions.

Alternatives to printed guide production
The first alternative to guide production is obviously not to
have any; and not just for economic reasons. Even some large
organizations eschew this form of information skills teaching.
Adhering to the principle that one-to-one teaching is the

most effective approach in teaching information skills, they argue that guide production does not stimulate the information or service user to make this personal approach, and so no guides, or perhaps one basic guide to the library, are produced. In the small library or information unit, where close personal contact is a normal feature of the service, then the guide might even be redundant. Some large libraries have a policy not to produce printed guides (not even a simple guide to the library's services) because they are unconvinced that they are read or used by those for whom they are produced. They may or may not be right, but there is very little evidence one way or the other. However, a study by Taylor (done in five inner London polytechnics) indicated that 'although the library guide is generally useful and informative, their [ie students] chief reason for not reading the guide is that they are not aware of its existence'.[1]

The second alternative is to have your guides prepared and produced for you — and at possibly little cost. This is by no means impossible, once you consider the point that preparing an information guide can itself be a most effective way of acquiring information and learning information skills. There may even be a nearby group which might find the *mechanics* of preparing an information guide a valuable exercise.

One example of this is in the school library context, where instead of just preparing a guide to the library for the children, they themselves might be asked to produce, as a team effort, an orientation guide. Clearly the fact that the exercise involves a wide variety of classroom skills means such an enterprise needs to be very carefully thought out, and in close cooperation with teaching staff. But potentially there are enormous benefits, not simply for the information skills programme but for the children in their other class work.

Another example could be applicable in any library context, but especially if you have links with or are close to a library school. In this case the library school student does not have the task of preparing a guide to the library and its services (although such an exercise would be interesting and valuable in his or her studies of library organization), but of preparing a guide to the literature of a specified subject or to a form of literature (eg standards, patents, etc). In other words it is an exercise in learning subject bibliography. In some library schools it is the preferred method of teaching the subject, and in the USA in the 1970s the preparation of subject guides or 'pathfinders' (these had no pretensions to being comprehensive bibliographies) were an important feature of bibliographic instruction in US academic libraries.

The third alternative is to use commercially-produced printed guides. For the most part this is not a viable alternative. Many examples are to be found in each of the categories listed at the beginning of this chapter.

Of the commercially-produced guides to the subject literature, few if any meet the needs of an information skills programme in any library or information unit. In spite of some of their claims to be useful to the student or teacher in the stated subject, they are, especially those published in the UK, generally too detailed and turgid for anyone other than the professional librarian or the student in library school training. There are exceptions, however, especially amongst those published in the USA, but the cost of multiple copies is generally prohibitive.

Likewise the cost of purchasing multiple copies of the much less numerous books on the various information skills would not be acceptable to the small organization.

But in the category of guides to specific reference materials there are some publishers which publish short, attractive guides to the use of some of their publications. These instructional guides often serve as promotional literature for the publications concerned. This in itself is not always a bad thing, but it usually means that the publication is a large and expensive one, and something which may not often be found in a small library or information unit. Thus the Institute for Scientific Information produces guides to the use of *Science citation index* and similar publications from its stable; BIOSIS produces guides to its abstracting services; and Encyclopaedia Britannica produces guides to its encyclopaedia. Occasionally, and just occasionally, a large publisher or more likely an organization with a vested interest in communication and information, altruistically publishes short guides which might be a valuable addition to an information skills programme — and distributes them free.

The fourth and final alternative to in-house production is a compromise (but a very good compromise): to use or if necessary adapt what has already been produced by another organization similar, if possible, to your own. The material may or may not have to be modified. The Library Instruction Materials Bank, established by the British Library Information Officer for User Education in Loughborough University of Technology, has over 10,000 printed guides, teaching handouts, etc on every conceivable aspect of information skills teaching, with many examples in every category. A sample collection of printed material is generally available on request, and after acknowledging the ideas or material you might have adapted from the original producer you could have an excellent guide on the subject you want.

The function of printed guides

If, having looked at the various alternatives, the decision is taken to produce a printed guide, you need to ask yourself a number of important questions. They should indeed be asked even before the subject of alternatives is considered. Broadly the questions deal with the purpose of printed guides, how they are to be used, and who they are meant for.

Firstly, there is the general and most important question of purpose, and inside this question there are three particular questions that need to be posed:

1 Is it intended to be promotional? Are you trying to sell the service? Are you trying to attract more use of your service?

2 Is it orientational? Are you attempting to describe the service and to guide your clientele around it?

3 Is it instructional? Is it a teaching instrument?

Secondly, there is the question of how it is to be used. Is it a self-explanatory, self-contained publication which can stand on its own, or must it be used in a special teaching context and supplemented by, say, a lecture or talk?

Thirdly, there is the question of whom it is meant for. Is it, for example, the first-year college student, or the final-year college student, or the experienced college lecturer? Each may have a different knowledge of the services, stock or skills, publicized, described or taught, and also your service may have different rules for different categories of users. The point is that the users of your guides belong to different groups with different needs and differing previous knowledge.

The above questions may seem to be obvious but perhaps because they are obvious they are infrequently asked or a clear answer is not always sought. Nevertheless they do need to be asked because this 'use' profile of the printed guide largely determines the features and style of the publication.

Many printed guides are mixtures of promotional, orientational and instructional guides, and they are often used in a variety of situations for a variety of different types of user. In a small library or information unit there may be a temptation to produce such a conglomerate, in the interests of economy. The temptation should be resisted. The right message at the right time is the soundest principle in information skills teaching, and it is achieved by responding precisely to the information user's specific needs. Printed guides which attempt to serve a number of purposes end up satisfying none.

At the beginning of this chapter printed guides were categorized in terms of their content, and in many respects this is a valid and convenient way of looking at printed materials. However, when it comes to the practical problem of producing guides, the categorization into promotional, orientational and instructional is the most useful, and this is how the production problem will be tackled here.

Promotional guides
Consider first of all the promotional guide. Promotional publications are produced primarily to convert the non-users of your service to become users. By definition these non-users will not be found in and around your service, so most of this material should be placed where your non-users and potential users are most likely to see it.

Everyone of us is bombarded by promotional literature every day, whether it is through our letterboxes or in the street, so we have built up a jaundiced attitude to this material. It is salutary to remember that before you take up the idea. In the context of the library and information field the effectiveness of the promotional leaflet has been put in doubt by the apparently negligible results of two recent promotional campaigns associated with public libraries.[2,3]

Your prospects of success could be enhanced if the visual quality of the promotional material is good. It must be smart, well-designed, and well-produced. The image you present in your promotional material might just determine the users' impression of your service. A scruffy leaflet, in their eyes, could reflect a scruffy service.

High-quality production can be expensive, but even if
your parent organization cannot provide the design and
production expertise, it ought to have some concern that
whatever you print should reflect well on itself. It's a long
shot, because if it has the money or the desire to spend
the money on you it would surely have spent it on your
service. Your prospects of a multi-colour, glossy poster or
leaflet are thus slim. The best advice is that if the final pro-
uct is likely to be less than first-rate, forget it.

Orientational guides

Orientational publications are to be found in most library
and information units, and it is in this area of printed matter
that probably all your efforts will lie. The emphasis here is
less on presentation and more on organization of the content.
The information in these guides should be presented concisely
and lucidly, and organized for quick and easy access by the
reader. He or she should not have to wade through several paragraphs or pages to find the information he or she wants. These
guides should inform without fuss and with the minimum of
effort on the part of the reader. Unfortunately, whatever
their skills in collecting and storing information, library and
information personnel tend to be weak in their presentation and communication of information, and the majority
of orientational guides are poorly organized, turgid and
cluttered with jargon. All too often it is a pamphlet of prose
that has to be read and sifted to get the required information;
and an index or contents list is a rarity.

Yet in recent years there has appeared quite a variety of
alternative and sometimes innovative formats, eg guides
produced as newspaper tabloids, guides organized as A-Z
directories, guides broken down into single-sheet leaflets,
with or without glossy wallets. There are four main reasons
for this change — financial economy, production convenience,
user needs, and the availability of some imaginative designers.
Each of these is a factor which you need to consider when
preparing a guide. Let's take three of these formats and
consider their suitability for you in terms of these factors.

Prose pamphlet

This traditional style of library guide, typeset and with
justified margins, has become an increasingly expensive

production — even if your parent organization has the facilities and they are available to you. You can economize by foregoing typesetting and opting for camera-ready typescript, but then it will need more paper and become much larger, and unless you have some imaginative typing the final product can look decidedly amateurish.

In terms of production convenience there are more problems. You may not have the difficult task of large libraries of coordinating the efforts of site librarians and/or section heads but it requires a concentrated effort to prepare one large guide for printing at a specific and perhaps very busy time of the year. And it can be particularly frustrating to realize that any change in services, etc will need to wait until another year before it can be incorporated in the guide. Yet to some extent the production and updating of the booklet guide has now been considerably eased by the advent of the word processor. If you have access to this valuable form of information technology, additions to and subtractions from the text are swift and easy.

Yet it is in convenient user access that the main failings of this form of guide lie. They are not inherent in the booklet format out of necessity, but it seems that librarian-produced guides tend to end up this way. They usually comprise paragraphs or sections describing layout, stock and services, and unless there is a decent contents list or index (which there rarely is) the entire booklet has to be scanned by the reader for the required information.

A-Z directory

This relatively uncommon format suffers from the same problems as the prose pamphlet in terms of production costs and to some extent production convenience, but in terms of user convenience it is a substantial improvement.

These A-Z directories are printed as booklets, sometimes very large ones, and they simply comprise a large number of brief, explanatory notes on the stock, services, facilities, etc within a library or information unit (see Figure 5 as an example).

Although they have the disadvantages of prose pamphlets in terms of the production convenience noted above, they are much easier to compile. It is the difference between writing, say, a two-page essay on the interlibrary loan service and highlighting the main features of this service and writing a sentence on each. The secret of compiling the A-Z directory is putting yourself in the shoes of the users and selecting a number of keywords (and their synonyms) or key topics which they will need to know about when they visit your service. Anyone with a good knowledge of user problems can put it together quite easily: just list the problems and the topics and write as briefly as possible on each. Prepared from the user's standpoint, the directory should be easily readable.

The loose-leaf wallet

The loose-leaf wallet is judged to be the best solution to the disadvantages of production convenience and user access associated with the prose pamphlet. A guide comprising several separate leaflets, each on a different library and information service, can be produced piecemeal, staggering the process throughout the year. Updating can then be continuous if required. As far as the user is concerned, instead of forcing him or her to wade through an unindexed booklet to find out, say, how to use the interlibrary loan system, it is much better to provide him or her with a single information sheet on that service. And a further advantage of this single-leaflet approach is that each leaflet can be made available wherever and whenever the user most needs it, that is, at the point-of-use or point-of-need. Thus a leaflet explaining the interlibrary loan system is placed at this service point where it is required, or a leaflet explaining how to use a particular set of reference books can be placed on the shelf nearby.

In a small library or information unit, where the variety of services or service points is not large, then a proliferation of leaflets is probably neither necessary nor economical, but the advantages of the flexibility and specificity of the single-leaflet approach are worth bearing in mind.

An example of an orientational guide

Figures 2-7 are extracts from a library guide produced many years ago by what was then a college of technology. The extracts are included here to illustrate, in one guide, the prose pamphlet guide, the A-Z guide, and the single-sheet guide. The guide is not offered as an ideal model for an orientational guide, but it does have several points of merit —

the existence of a contents page (Figure 2) and the simplicity and brevity of the text.

Pages 5-6 (Figure 3) are parts of the guide which describe in simple prose briefly and concisely the library's services and stock. Pages 19-27 (Figures 5-7) form an A-Z guide to the library with much the same information (even more concisely written) as pages 5-6 (and onwards), but re-organized as an alphabetical directory (an expanded index if you like). Pages 10-11 on book loans (Figure 4) could form the single-sheet guide to that service.

Considered as a whole this guide more than adequately meets the requirements of orientational guides suggested earlier — 'the information in these guides should be presented concisely and lucidly, and organized for quick and easy access by the reader'. The reader in this case has three points of access to the information contained in the guide — through the list of contents, through the prose text of the guide, and through the A-Z directory. This choice suits the different preferences of different readers, and to the reader in a hurry or who cannot match the terms of his or her enquiry to the jargon of the library or information unit. This guide may not be the most visually exciting one ever produced, but it gives versatile and economical access to the information.

Instructional guides

In the case of instructional guides, presentation (ie design qualities) matter least of all; although if it is to be made generally available within the library or information unit as opposed to being just offered as a class teaching handout, some effort should be made to make it attractive. Organization is important, but the information content matters most of all.

Instructional guides cover three main categories:
1 Guides to the subject literature
2 Guides to specific reference materials
3 Guides to information techniques

In large academic libraries, an enormous and disporportionate effort is put into compiling them. Unfortunately the end result usually appears to meet the requirements of a bibliographical exercise at library school, rather than the needs of the student user. This, in fairness, generally applies only to the category of guides to the subject literature, and this is a category which few small libraries and information units are

LIBRARY
GUIDE

BATTERSEA COLLEGE
OF TECHNOLOGY

CONTENTS

2

Figure 2

LOCATION AND LAYOUT

The Library is situated to the left of the main entrance on the ground floor.

The entrance-hall to the Library contains the issue-desk, the catalogues, directories and encyclopaedias.

There are three reading-rooms : —

OLD LIBRARY, which contains mainly the bound volumes and back files of journals.

NEW LIBRARY, in which is shelved the bookstock relating to science and technology, and also the current issues of journals.

SOCIAL SCIENCES READING-ROOM, housing the books in this field.

A plan of the Library is on the centre pages.

5

Figure 3

STOCK

There are about 30,000 books, pamphlets and bound journals, principally in the fields of the sciences and technologies. A programme of expansion is under way and during the current year we expect to add about 8,000 items.

With the exception of journals and reference books, all the material is available for loan (*see* Rules and regulations).

BOOKS

Books in the fields of science and technology are shelved in the New Library, with an overflow into the Old Library; those relating to the social sciences are housed in their own reading-room.

The arrangement on the shelves is by subject, which is indicated by a number on the spine. This subject number determines the order (*see* Classification).

The catalogue is located in the Entrance Hall.

6

BOOK LOANS

BORROWING

4 books may be borrowed at any one time. Books are lent for 14 days.

A book loan form must be filled in for each book.

RENEWALS

Books may be renewed by personal application at the Issue Desk, by post, or by telephone, quoting the book number and the date of return.

Books may be renewed once only by quoting the book number, after which the book itself must be produced before a further renewal can be given.

A book will NOT be renewed if it has been requested by another reader.

REFERENCE BOOKS AND JOURNALS

These are for use in the Library only. *Subject to the Librarian's discretion*, certain reference

10

Figure 4

books may be borrowed after 4.30 p.m. each day for return by 10 a.m. the next day.

Abstract journals, quick-reference books, manuals and handbooks are never lent in this way.

STAFF

Special regulations apply for staff. Please ask at the Issue Desk.

11

A ... B ... C GUIDE

BOOKS are shelved by subject, *see* CLASSIFIC-
ATION.

You may borrow up to 4 books.

BORROWING *see* LOANS.

CASES, BAGS, etc., may NOT be brought into
the Library. Racks are provided.

CATALOGUE of books is maintained on cards
in the ENTRANCE HALL. This shows which
books the library has by a given author or on
a given subject.

There is also an *Index of theses*.

CLASSIFICATION. Books are arranged by subject, each with its subject number. A key to the
main subject numbers is given in this booklet.

19

Figure 5

COPYING. We offer a document-copying service at 6d. per foolscap sheet. Ask for details at the ISSUE DESK.

ENQUIRY DESK is in the OLD LIBRARY. All enquiries about the literature should be made here.

EXAMINATION PAPERS are filed in the OLD LIBRARY. There are sets of University of London, Institution and Dip. Tech. papers for loan. Reference copies of papers are shelved in QUICK REFERENCE.

FINES of 1d. per day are charged on each book retained after the date of return.

ISSUE DESK is immediately inside the EN-TRANCE HALL. Books are issued and returned here.

Forms for books loans, requests and copying are in the ENTRANCE HALL and OLD LIBRARY.

20

JOURNALS are filed in 3 sequences : —
1. The current issue is in the NEW LIBRARY.
2. The current year's file is in the GALLERY.
3. Back runs are shelved in fixed locations.
The *Index of Journals* shows every journal held by the library, with its location.

LOANS. Books may be borrowed for 2 weeks and renewed for a further period if not required by another reader.
The date of return is stamped in the book. A separate form must be filled in for each book borrowed.

MEMBERSHIP. As a student of the College you are a member of the College library. There are no further forms to fill in—except the form for borrowing a book.

MICROCARD and MICROFILM READERS are available for the use of readers in the OLD LIBRARY. Some of the library's holdings of journals are on microcard.

21

Figure 6

OPENING TIMES
  Monday to Friday,
    TERM   9 a.m.—8.30 p.m.
    VACATION   9 a.m.—5 p.m.

PERIODICALS *see* JOURNALS.

QUICK REFERENCE books, including encyclopaedias and directories, are shelved in the
  ENTRANCE HALL.

RENEW your books on loan for a further 2-week
  period by personal application at the ISSUE
  DESK, by post, or by telephone (MAC 9191,
  Ext. 13). We need to know the book number
  and the date due.

  A book will NOT be renewed if requested by
  another reader.

REQUESTS for books or journals must be made
  out on the forms provided, one for each request.

22

We offer the following service : —

Any student may request a book which is in the library stock but not on the shelves.

Research students and final year students may request material not held by the library.

A fee of 3d. is charged for each request card.

SILENCE is requested in all parts of the library.

STAFF are here to help you. If you cannot find what you want, ask at the ENQUIRY DESK.

TAPE-RECORDER is available for use in the library.

TEXTBOOKS. We have one or two copies of most standard textbooks, but these are in constant use. Public libraries and London University Library may also have copies. Better still, buy your own, especially in the first year.

23

Figure 7

THESES. A copy is held of each higher degree thesis taken at the College. Theses are strictly for reference in the library only and must be asked for at the ISSUE DESK.

There is an *Index of theses* with the book catalogue.

or ought to be tempted into, even in the smaller college library. Remember that your courses are more vocationally-orientated rather than academical. But if you do find yourself preparing such guides, then note that the primary objective is to guide the user through the maze of literature on a specific subject. It is not enough to list the available literature, grouping it into sections by form (reports, encyclopaedias, dictionaries, directories, conference proceedings, etc). The average library and information users rarely come with an information problem neatly packaged by form, and even if they do they still need to be guided through perhaps a selection of, to them, rather similar and equally useful information sources. They need to be able to identify the most suitable information source, and, if possible, to have some notion of the reliability, the currency, etc of that source to them. If the function of a guide to the subject literature is looked at from this point of view, it is clear that the typical subject guide produced by academic libraries for general distribution is not a satisfactory answer to the users' information problems.

The librarian's task in the subject guide should be to guide the user through a choice of possible information sources, pointing out the level and quality of information in the source, and the strengths and weaknesses of the source. Each source in the guide needs to be critically annotated and evaluated, and analytically indexed — the usual bare description of the contents of each source really is not enough.

As has already been noted, subject guides to the literature abound in university and polytechnic libraries, and although none in particular can be wholly recommended, some could be amended and modified, but the task could be so big that your efforts in guiding the library and information user should go elsewhere.

Guides to specific reference books are also to be found in profusion, emanating from a variety of library and information environments, and sometimes even the publishers of the books themselves. There is a limit to the number of variations these guides can take, though you could devote just one page to the use of the *Encyclopaedia Britannica* instead of six, or you could concentrate more on its weaknesses than its strengths. The many guides already produced on these different reference books already cover many of the alternative approaches, so it is unnecessary for you to start from scratch. It is better to gather samples of what is available, and make a composite guide which suits your local circumstances — the needs of your users in using these reference works.

A similar approach can be taken with the last category of instructional guide — the guide to information skills techniques. The basic principles of, say, search strategies or evaluating an information source or note-taking from lectures don't differ substantially from one sector to another, unless in terms of depth or the type of information user, so a selection of what has been prepared by other library and information units could be used. But don't forget that all these skills have been described, listed, illustrated and discussed in innumerable books, and photocopying (with permission of course) relevant pages might do as well as anything.

Conclusion

In concluding this chapter it would have been valuable to give a detailed checklist of dos and don'ts in the matter or printed guides. Some advice and illustrations have been given, and the temptation is to offer more. But there is a lack of serious, non-descriptive research into information skills teaching through printed guides, and especially on research on the reactions of users to this form of instruction and orientation.

One exception is some of the work done by Mayes on the readability of printed library guides. As a by-product of this work he printed a leaflet entitled *39 steps by which you can improve your library publications.*[4] Although one can quibble with some of the suggestions and seek further evidence to support the points he makes, he gives many sensible pointers to better printed guides, and these are just a few:

No 1   Spend a little time thinking about who is going to read your publication. What do these people really want to know?

No 2   Grit your teeth and ask your staff for their opinion on your publication.

No 7   Avoid jargon unless it is absolutely necessary.

No 8   It is depressing but true that good printing and graphics impress the customers. Use the best you can get. If your facilities are extremely primitive, perhaps it would be better not to go into print.

No 12 Start with a paragraph/sentence that will grab the reader's attention.

No 21 Always use one short word where one long word would have done.

No 28 It may seem obvious, but words of common use ('high frequency' words) make for more readable writing.

References

1 Taylor, Heather *An investigation into student and staff attitudes towards library guides in a sample of polytechnic libraries.* Master of Library Studies Thesis, Loughborough University of Technology, 1980.

2 Woodhouse, Roger G, and Neill, J *The promotion of public library use: an experiment in promotion and a national survey of activities.* Newcastle upon Tyne, Newcastle upon Tyne Polytechnic Department of Librarianship, 1978 (BLR&DD Report No 5470).

3 Cronin, Blaise *Direct mail advertising and public library use.* London, British Library Board, 1980 (BLR&DD Report No 5539).

4 Mayes, Paul B *39 steps by which you can improve your library publications.* 1979 (Unpublished pamphlet).

Chapter Eleven

Evaluation

No other facet of information skills instruction causes as much concern, theorizing, confusion, controversy and despair as evaluation. Perhaps because of this, evaluation, in its formal sense, is largely avoided in all sectors. Even where it is initiated it is often abandoned through lack of support of those being evaluated, and where the effort has been sustained to the end the results of the evaluation are treated with some circumspection.

There are arguments for and against formal evaluation. The case against it is supported by reasons such as your lack of time, your lack of knowledge of techniques, programme participants will not like it or misinterpret it, teachers rarely have their teaching evaluated, and other parts of the library or information service are not evaluated. On the other hand there are a number of consequences of there being no evaluation — you cannot tell if the best teaching methods are being applied or if you are any good at using them, and above all you cannot tell if the programme is broadly a success or a failure. Thus the sound reasons for formal evaluation seem to be counterbalanced by strong practical problems which seem to obstruct it.

Not all evaluation need be formal, however, and in fact informal evaluation (though it may not be given even this descriptor) is exercised in almost every programme of information skills. If your programme goes wrong you will try to find out why and how and perhaps change it; if your information users do not like tape-slide media then you try something else, and so on. This sort of informal and non-explicit evaluation is as valid and useful as formal evaluation with its sophisticated methodologies.

In the small library or information unit, therefore, you will do some evaluation consciously or otherwise. A full-scale, formal evaluation of the entire programme in all its dimensions is almost certainly beyond your resources, even if you can draw upon the results of self-evaluation techniques implanted in some of the teaching modes of the programme, and the results of evaluation by external evaluators. Yet much can be done by informal evaluation and the objective of this chapter is to emphasize this and highlight where it arises in the programme and how it can be used. In the planning and preparation of a programme the groundwork is prepared (sometimes incidentally) for much evaluation data to emerge; what you need to do is to harness this data and use it for the improvement of the programme.

What do you evaluate?

It is very easy to become overwhelmed and confused by the mass of evaluation data, and the solution is broadly to categorize the various things you are evaluating. The four most important are as follows:

1 Evaluating learned outcomes
2 Evaluating learning outcomes
3 Evaluating teaching methods and modes
4 Evaluating the programme as a whole.

Evaluating learning outcomes

Evaluating learning outcomes means determining whether or not the participants in the programme achieved what they set out to do or what was set out for them to do. It is the most important area of evaluation, and fortunately there is more than one way of getting the information.

The first approach is to go back to the statement of aims and objectives. Take the example we considered in the chapter on that topic. Did the first-year pupils at secondary school X, by the end of the first year, have the necessary information skills to plan, research and write class assignments and projects at a level acceptable to their teachers? The key phrase in this case is 'at a level acceptable to their teachers', and three points arise from this example. Firstly, the criterion for success was measured in qualitative terms not quantitative terms. Secondly, the final arbiter of success or failure was the teacher. Thirdly, the burden of evaluation lay with the teacher not the librarian. These points do not apply on every occasion (for example, the measurement could be in quantitative terms, or your opinion or the student's opinion could be agreed as equally valid), but clearly evaluation is as much a joint enterprise as the setting of mutually-acceptable objectives was, so the onus does not lie entirely on you.

The advantages of this first approach to evaluation are, firstly, if the programme objectives are properly set then the evaluation of the learning outcome follows almost automatically (in other words evaluation is built into the stage of setting objectives); and secondly, *all* parties in the programme are aware of the criteria of success or failure at the outset.

These two merits are even more evident in the special case of information skills teaching by self-instructional methods. If the programmed learning technique is used (using a workbook for example), evaluation is effected as the programme continues, because in order to finish the programme the participant must have given satisfactory answers to all the questions. The computer-assisted instruction mode provides even more evaluation data if it can store information on the frequency and nature of incorrect responses.

A second approach to evaluating learning outcomes is to use the pre-test and post-test method. It is used in schools in teaching some other subjects and skills, and it has been used for library skills, although current thinking on information skills does not favour it. Elsewhere in colleges and other parts of higher education it is uncommon. In simplest terms you get a baseline of knowledge (measured before the instruction begins by a pre-test) and then you test the students after the instruction (with a post-test) to determine what change in their knowledge has occurred.

There are disadvantages in this method, and two of the most important are, first, that the change in knowledge may arise from learning experiences unconnected with your instruction; and second, that you are testing acquired knowledge and not techniques. Yet this sort of evaluation does have its advantages: first, the pre-test can be a method of learning in its own right in that students may foresee the scope of the skills they should acquire; and second, the pre-test can illuminate for you their information skills needs.

Although pre-testing and post-testing is not common, the setting of practical work as part of the instruction programme is widespread. These are question-and-answer exercises for the most part and can be regarded as post-tests. They are used primarily to give the student practice in techniques just taught but they are obviously as valuable in providing information on the effectiveness of your instruction. If you can build into the exercise the requirement that the respondent notes how and where the answer was got, as well as the answer itself, then you go some way towards evaluating techniques as well as knowledge.

Evaluating learning experiences

Evaluating learning experiences means determining the reaction of your programme participants to one part of the instruction they have been given or to the programme as a whole.

It is in this area of evaluation that formal evaluation most often gives way to informal evaluation, qualitative evaluation all but replaces quantitative evaluation, and 'hard' evaluation becomes 'soft' evaluation. Nevertheless this 'soft', informal evaluation should not be undervalued. Moreover formal approaches using quantitative techniques are generally inappropriate here; you are looking for opinion and feedback and this comes more easily through informal approaches. This evaluation is by no means easy — opinion can be influenced by attitude, participants may not have anything to measure your programme against, and how do you know you are getting the honest reaction rather than the non-committed or 'okay' response?

Your main approach will be to ask the participants what they thought of the instruction — (formally) by questionnaire, or (less formally) by interview, or (informally) by casually asking their opinions. The questionnaire is quick, convenient, and can be consistently used with all participants. On the other hand it can condition responses, it can be impersonal, it does not always draw out other useful information, and (a non-trivial point) somehow you have to ensure that you get it back. Interviews using a prepared questionnaire remove the disadvantages of the questionnaire on its own but can you afford the enormous extra time required? Finally, there is the casual sampling of opinion. This is quick, convenient, person-to-person, and it can bring out unexpected points, but how do you select those you seek opinions from, how do you consistently ask the same questions, and how do you retain the opinions you get for later consideration?

There is a further, more important problem in evaluating learning experiences. If you solicit a response immediately after the instruction then everything is fresh in their minds and you will get a fairly clear idea of their views of the learning experience ('Yes, it met my needs', and 'No, I didn't know any of this before'). What you will not get is a considered view of how relevant and ultimately useful your instruction is. You get this and other information (for example, 'the timing was right/wrong') from later questioning, but by this time the actual learning has become vague in recollection. The solution is to take opinions both immediately after and also some time after the instruction.

Another, yet not necessarily an alternative approach to evaluating learning experiences is to invite someone to sit in on your instruction and observe the proceedings. If you are team-teaching then this option is immediately at hand — one teacher teaches while the other observes the participants' reactions. Not only does this observational approach estimate the learning experience, albeit indirectly, it also permits some assessment of your respective teaching performances. The disadvantages are, firstly, that it can be difficult to record and collate the observed activities of the programme participants; and secondly, it may not be easy for the team individually to stand back and look at the instruction dispassionately.

This question of objectivity is a major difficulty in evaluation, not only from the instructor's standpoint but also from the students' viewpoint — in the students' eyes evaluation is often misinterpreted as being the investigation of their performance rather than the investigation of the value of the programme and its teaching. The solution, and often it is a very successful one in terms of getting students to respond and co-operate, is to bring in an outside, professional evaluator. The advantages are that you save your time, the evaluators are experts (or they should be), they are independent and uninvolved, and most important they are seen to be independent by the programme participants.

Evaluating teaching methods and modes

This is a common area of evaluation in the literature of information skills appearing frequently in earnest librarianship theses. From the results of this research there is no consistent and conclusive evidence that any one teaching method or mode works better than another. There is a similar lack of evidence in teaching beyond information skills teaching. All this is hardly surprising, because, as was noted in earlier chapters, each method and mode has advantages and disadvantages. Your (good or bad) videotape (badly- or well-presented) simply may have weighted the 'advantages' or 'disadvantages' end of the see-saw, and all your evaluation may do is to reflect this. There is also evidence that individual students have different learning styles and sometimes because of this they will respond better to some teaching methods and modes than to others.

Therefore it is hardly worthwhile putting any effort into this area of evaluation in any way other than the most informal. But even a basic, opinion-seeking question on, say, the value of the videotape, will give you many interesting answers. So how can you meaningfully interpret this information for the ultimate benefit of the programme? This highlights the purpose of evaluation. You will gather a lot of information and data, yet it is little value unless you can use it and interpret it with confidence to change and hence improve the programme.

Evaluating the programme as a whole

Having gathered all the evaluation information and data on learning outcomes, learning experiences, teaching methods and teaching modes, you might think that that is sufficient to make an overall assessment of the programme. Possibly so, but you should not ignore the wealth of other statistical data that you can add. The answers to questions like how many hours you have taught, how many programme participants were involved, and how often you were approached for teaching duties, are all relevant, and if you have data such as the increased (or decreased) use of the information service then this too is valuable. If you have comparable figures from previous years then this data is even more meaningful.

What you have then is probably an enormous accumulation of opinions, results, data, perhaps examination marks, etc from programme participants, external evaluation, other teachers and yourself. How do you make sense of this plethora of confusing and possibly conflicting information? There is, I am afraid, no simple answer to this. The paradox is that the more information you gather the hazier the picture of your programme may become.

The best advice is as follows. Decide what information and data is essential. Appraise what is likely to be the most reliable. Gather the data carefully and interpret it as you go along. Consider the different areas of evaluation like learning outcomes and learning experiences more or less discretely, until all the information and data you feel is necessary has been gathered, and only then make an assessment of the overall value of the programme. Assuredly not all aspects of your programme will be successful, yet the primary intention of evaluation is not to pronounce success or failure, but to highlight success and failure within the programme and amend and improve where necessary.

Conclusion

After all this, is the time and effort you spend on evaluation justified in your situation of limited resources? Certainly it is. It is because you have limited resources that it is important not to squander them on activities which are ineffectual. You can only determine whether resources spent on information skills teaching are wasted if you evaluate the programme.

Chapter Twelve

Timing and frequency

Timing

The timing of information skills instruction is regarded as one of the keys to success or failure in a programme. The argument goes like this: the basic principle is that the nature and content of a programme should be determined by the real needs of the library and information user. If the needs and requirements of the user are thus paramount, then it would seem that you should react as and when these needs become apparent, in other words whenever he or she has an information problem. Thus you offer information skills instruction whenever the user has an information problem. There are several points to make about this argument.

Firstly, you need to be fully aware and preferably able to anticipate when information problems arise and will arise amongst your users. This means that you have to have a good knowledge of day-to-day working in your organization. In a small library or information unit this is much easier than in a large unit, because of your close contact with your clientele.

Secondly, even when you are on the spot when the problem arises, it may well be impractical to drop everything to do your bit of instruction. Even notice of a couple of weeks can be far too short.

Thirdly, the best and most appropriate response to a user's information problem is not always instruction. Frequently it is the information itself, not the wherewithall to get the information. The clever librarian sometimes manages to balance information provision with information instruction, but the clever librarian also knows that it is often a matter of fine judgment; knowing when is the appropriate time to offer instruction and when it is the time to provide information, and knowing what proportion of which to offer.

This basic principle of offering instruction only when the need is apparent has therefore to be qualified. Just bear in mind that it might be most effective at this stage. It may be the most relevant and effective time, but it may not be the most appropriate or convenient.

But if the problem of good timing is a sensitive one, then the problem of bad timing is a delicate one. I noted that it may be bad timing to offer the user information skills instruction when he or she really needs the information itself. This applies particularly in the one-to-one, off-the-cuff situation. In the case of dealing with groups, the common example of bad timing is to offer instruction not just when no information problem has arisen, but when the users have no conception that they have any information problems at all. This arises frequently in the first few days or weeks of the students' arrival at college. Many college libraries schedule orientation tours of the library at this time. If you admit that all that is possible at this time is to foster a feeling in the students that the library is a useful, helpful place, and give only some basic orientation, then this is adequate. But if you try to offer some in-depth instruction, either then or within a very short time afterwards, then failure should be expected. The simple reason is that students are unlikely to have encountered any information problems that require skills instruction at that time.

Unfortunately in the case of students just beginning the college year, it happens to be the time when their lecturers have most free slots on the timetable for their students. The various courses have not really moved into gear and there are gaps in the timetable, gaps which, they believe, might just suit the librarian and his or her information skills course. The librarian given such an opportunity has a dilemma: does he or she accept the slots and face the probability that the students will not be interested or motivated because they cannot see the relevance of such instruction at that time? Or does the librarian decline the offer, thus possibly offending the lecturer, and resigning himself or herself to the chance that the offer will not come again or at best will come very late in the student's career? There is no clear answer to this, but the keys to it lie partly in your relationship with the lecturer concerned and partly in the nature of your information skills programme.

Firstly, if you have done the groundwork for the programme carefully and made the lecturer aware of what you are trying to do and what relation it has to the curriculum, then in the majority of cases you will not be put into this predicament. If your programme has been prepared so that it is an accepted and integral part of the whole curriculum, then the teaching staff will appreciate the fact that proper timing is essential, not just from your point of view but his.

The second key is the nature of your programme. I indicated that the information needs of the library and information user are paramount, and earlier I made the distinction between information needs and information *skills* needs. If we consider that your programme is a response to information skills needs, it is clear that there are two sorts, namely short-term needs and long-term needs. To illustrate this take the situation in colleges, where students have the short-term aims of preparing the next project and the long-term aims of entering the career of their choice and being successful. Likewise, in a school the pupil's short-term aims are to complete the next assignment, and the long-term aims might be entering higher education and doing well there. In both cases we could insert medium-term aims like passing the final examinations.

In order to meet these aims some information skills will be necessary; and just as there is a relationship between those aims, there is, or should be, a relationship between short-term, medium-term and long-term information skills needs. Furthermore you have a responsibility to ensure that the information skills you teach in order to meet short-term aims are also necessary to meet long-term aims, and that you do justify their premature teaching, if you do teach information skills which will only be useful in the long-term.

It is therefore possible to devise programmes which include long-term information skills as well as short-term information skills. It need not be either one or the other, but you must explain this and justify it to your target group of users. Once you decide that the programme will comprise long-term and short-term skills, the question of timing becomes less crucial.

Frequency

One of the great credos in information skills instruction is that it should be continuous. It is for this reason that many library and information personnel prefer a programme which is spread over a few months rather than a blockbuster which fills a number of consecutive days. It also increases the possibility of relating the programme to the everyday activities of the target users. But just as important is the opportunity, not just to introduce new skills, but to reinforce earlier ones.

An information skill can be compared to learning to ride a bicycle. One lesson on riding the bicycle is rarely sufficient: the technique can be explained, your teacher will keep you upright, and you get a little practice. You might get the hang of it after an hour or so, but if you don't ride the bicycle for a few months you will have lost the technique and fall off. You need practice. Similarly, information skills are acquired and absorbed by practice and reinforcement. The librarian need not always be at hand — what you need is practice.

Many programmes include practice in the skills, usually question-and-answer search strategies. This gives immediate practice and reinforcement, but unless this practice can be continued in everyday activities, skills will disappear.

Chapter Thirteen

Cooperation

Introduction
Throughout the book so far, cooperation, if not always explicitly referred to, has been implicit. Its value in the small library and information unit is such, however, that it needs to be examined as an issue in its own right.

Although it manifests itself in many different ways, there are broadly two kinds of cooperation: firstly, there is the cooperation that you need from within your organization to enable you to develop and operate your programme, and secondly, there is the cooperation that you should seek from agencies outside your organization.

Cooperation from within
It may seem superfluous to say so (especially in a small library), but you have to have the cooperation and support of all library and information staff at all stages of the preparation and implementation of the programme. This ought to mean not just passive acceptance of the programme, but some degree of enthusiasm for it. Ideally it should be a combined effort between all staff, but some may not want to teach or even be involved in the programme. In the latter situation, care should be taken to ensure that full information about the programme is provided or available at all times. Cooperation is a two-way process, so if you rely on the cooperation of your own staff to support your programme, they will expect to be kept informed of developments that may significantly affect other parts of the service for which they are responsible.

Important though the above cooperation is, the crucial issue is cooperation between you and other members of the organization, who may or may not be your targets for instruction. Without this support and cooperation even a programme which is concerned solely with basic library skills will have limited or no success. In a more broadly-based information skills programme the prospects of success are nil.

This cooperation takes many forms: for example, information on possible targets for the programme, information on their information skills needs, agreement on aims and objectives, agreement on programme content, possibly and hopefully the sharing of the teaching load, help on the availability of teaching resources and equipment and contributions to the evaluation process. Clearly the cooperation and involvement should take place at every stage of the programme, from its initiation to its evaluation.

The advantages of close cooperation are many, including
1 It ensures the relevance of the programme
2 It improves the motivation in the target group
3 It indicates what is possible in terms of resources
4 The implications of the programme on the remainder of the organization become more evident
5 Mutual respect and awareness

To illustrate these advantages it is appropriate to consider the schools, colleges, public libraries and special libraries in turn.

Schools

No information skills programme is possible in a school unless there is proper cooperation between the librarian and the teacher. One or two hours of basic library skills instruction might be possible with little cooperation, but the bulk of the information skills programme requires full cooperation, even though in this case you have to accept that the end result may be that the largest part of the information skills instruction is done by the teachers.

Like cooperation in the other sectors it must begin at the beginning, so that there is mutual awareness and respect of aims and objectives and capabilities; so that if the teaching load is to be shared the proportion and responsibilities can be mapped out; and so that the implications for other teaching in the school can be determined. Through the programme of information skills (and this makes cooperation a long-term commitment) cooperation must be maintained and be seen to be maintained. Pupils are more likely to accept the importance of information skills if they see such cooperation. In other words they are better motivated.

Colleges
The dual function of the tutor-librarian in colleges as teacher and librarian should be an asset in cooperation, although this double role can sometimes mean that the information skills programme is left largely to the librarian. Frequently there is a dichotomy between the two wings of information skills (library skills and study and communication skills) because the tutor-librarians and teaching staff teaching study skills each regard themselves as specialists.

Nevertheless there is cooperation in the colleges and it is being stimulated by outside-validated courses like TEC and BEC, which increasingly require broad information skills elements to be taught in their courses.

Public libraries
Although many courses that are run in this sector are independent of any group outside the library system, courses involving two target groups (schoolchildren and adult education groups) have to struggle unless they have cooperation from outside.

For instance, public library programmes for schoolchildren may be limited in scope unless the teachers supply the information that the librarians need to make the programme relevant: for example, details of current assignments which require use of public library resources. And the teacher's support is needed to motivate the pupils. If there is no cooperation then the librarian has to rely entirely on novelty of presentation and content.

In the case of adult education or adult learning courses the target group's motivation is usually very high, but the cooperation of the organizers of these courses is needed in the first place to put the public library programme into the course.

Special libraries
Cooperation is least evident in special libraries though it does underlie the programmes that are mounted. Being usually without an educational function the other personnel in the

special librarian's organization have no obvious interest in cooperating in an information skills programme. But at the same time the organization's primary aim as far as information is concerned is to see that the library and information unit provides a specialist information service, primarily direct information provision. Implicitly, therefore, without the consent if not the cooperation of the organization an information skills programme probably cannot be initiated.

Cooperation from outside

If your resources are limited in terms of both finance and manpower (and they are bound to be in a small unit), then you can either argue the case for more assistance from within your organization, or go outside your organization and seek assistance elsewhere.

Financial resources are unlikely to be forthcoming, although there is just the possibility that your proposed programme is of sufficient novelty or originality that it might warrant the description of being 'experimental'. In recent years the British Library Research and Development Department (BLR&DD) has invested large sums of money on user education (primarily concerned with library skills). Initially most of the work that was funded was done in universities and polytechnics; latterly attention has been transferred to schools and the scope of the work has been broadened to encompass information skills. As far as colleges of further and higher education, and public and special libraries are concerned, the general absence of research funding on information skills can be accounted for by the lack of adequate proposals for research, rather than by deliberate discrimination against these sectors. The BLR&DD is well aware of the interesting and varying circumstances that obtain in these sectors with regard to information skills, and some tentative enquiries are worth making.

The use of manpower resources from outside the organization is another possibility. It is not such an unusual step to take. For example, university, polytechnic, public and some college libraries have in the past lent support to information skills teaching in schools, either by organizing programmes within their institutions or, less frequently admittedly, by sending staff into the schools. Such a pair of hands is not only useful, it can bring a valuable extra dimension to your programme, as well as stimulating that most desirable of goals in information skills ideology — the continuity of information skills across all levels of education and beyond.

Don't forget the use of personnel from commercial organizations, although this possibility is only likely to be available for special libraries and perhaps colleges. The range of skills is narrowed to those that relate to new information techniques like on-line database searching. This service, quite often free, is offered by large database producers (usually) and host system operators. The problems here are, first, that you probably do not subscribe to the services they offer, and second, their ultimate aim is naturally to sell their product — user education is not just an alternative term for information skills instruction, it has its own marketing connotation.

Teaching support within any one sector, for example between two small colleges, is rare, but this is a possibility that could be investigated. Certainly there are problems, but to see what might be achieved just consider the analogy of the situation of small farmers at harvest-time not so long ago. They pooled their resources of manpower and equipment at a critical time to do a job of work that they would have struggled to do independently. So it is for the small college library or any other small information unit.

Cooperation which falls short of actual exchange of teaching personnel is quite common though not as widespread as many would like to see. Some of this cooperation comes as the result of organized conferences, meetings and seminars, where an exchange of experience and expertise is fostered. There have been many of these concerned with library skills in recent years, primarily for school, college, polytechnic, university and public libraries. The value of these is usually short-lived unless the meetings take place within a small region and there is the opportunity of regular and easy contact, or there is publication of the results, papers, etc of the meeting and this is well-disseminated throughout the region.

Some of this cooperation comes through the workings of small regional networks specializing in the teaching of information skills. It would be nice to recommend a selection of these different sectors in different regions, but their active lifetime tends to be short and although there are currently one or two in operation they are likely to have disappeared within a few months.

What has survived so far, and is scheduled to remain in existence until 1985 at least, is the British Library Information Officer for User Education Project based at Loughborough University of Technology. In spite of its location in a university it is a national service accessible to all library and information sectors and the teaching profession — in fact anyone with an interest in information skills. Part of its function is to provide a base or network through which personnel from all sectors can input and withdraw information and material relating to the teaching of information skills. This information and materials exchange offers a further tier of service in the form of advice and some practical help. Two of the primary reasons for the establishment of the project were to help break down the isolation of libraries and information units and hence to remove the 're-inventing the wheel' syndrome.

Chapter Fourteen

The skills and techniques you need

The skills
Most library and information personnel bring to the traditional library skills programme all the training they received in library school and all the experience and expertise they acquire through working in a library or information unit. Together this is sufficient to teach library skills.

For an information skills programme, with the scope envisaged here, this is not enough. Some of the techniques of study skills and communication skills, or the retrieval, organization, evaluation and communication of information are not taught in most library schools, though they can be picked up as a by-product of study at the institution of which the library school is part: library schools are still by and large primarily concerned with libraries and library techniques rather than the broader world of information and associated information techniques. Nor does experience in most libraries or information units provide expertise or practice in many of the information skills.

All this sounds part of the argument for library and information personnel confining information skills programmes to purely library techniques. The case against this narrow scope has already been argued elsewhere in this book. Here I have to try and help you overcome this problem.

First of all there has been an assumption or at least a hope that this information skills programme is to be planned and executed in conjunction with teachers, lecturers, or other educational personnel. Their expertise on some information skills, for example, report-writing, essay-writing, note-taking, etc can complement your particular area of expertise, for example, search strategies, using indexes, etc.

Secondly, if this complementary input of information skills from educational personnel is not available, you have two options. The first is to use audiovisual materials specially prepared for teaching specific information skills: this is partly why a whole chapter has been devoted to the use of audiovisual materials and sometimes lengthy descriptions given of their content. The second option is to learn these techniques yourself. This may seem a tall order, but it is not such an enormous task. The principles of many information skills (for example, note-taking from books or lectures) are basically simple common sense threaded together with a number of tips and short-cuts. Too often the techniques seem so obvious that students don't feel they have to make a special effort to learn them. Knowing how to use these techniques is only part of the story; the secret of acquiring and learning these techniques is to practise them. And that is done by those being taught, not by those teaching them. So what you have to do as the teacher is to know the techniques, pass them on to those being taught and try to ensure that the right environment is available to those being taught in which they can learn and develop these techniques. If it is not available then you have to consider whether these particular techniques should have been taught at that time.

Teaching techniques
There has always been some debate amongst librarians involved in library skills programmes on the need or otherwise for them to be taught teaching techniques. The argument on the one hand is that if you are trained to teach you will be a better teacher. There is a large element of truth in this but it is not entirely irrefutable. Nevertheless, the range of teaching methods and modes usually applied in library skills is so wide that some at least of these techniques have to be acquired somehow or another.

The argument from the other side is variously: (in colleges) teaching staff don't have to train as teachers so why should we, (in schools) if I had wanted to learn teaching techniques I would have trained as a teacher, (everywhere) there isn't the time or the training available. These are of course not reasoned arguments but excuses for not acquiring teaching techniques.

If you have the time, and if you have the training facilities nearby, then it is well worth taking some form of teaching training, no matter how brief it is. These are the best arguments for its acquisition:

1 Although acquiring teaching techniques does not necessarily imply that you will be an excellent teacher, it is almost certainly true that your programme will suffer if your teaching technique is bad.
2 If you do acquire some teaching training you are more likely to gain the respect of teaching colleagues with whom you are involved on the programme.
3 It does no harm these days to add to your skills, whether they are teaching or otherwise.

Unfortunately in many organizations, large or small, the facilities for acquiring teaching and training skills are small. Some colleges offer short (perhaps just one day) courses on audiovisual teaching, small-group tutoring, lecturing, etc but they are few and far between. If they are made available, get on to as many as possible. Not only are they usually free and excellently organized but they permit useful lecturer contact in a learning situation. Many public libraries organize staff-training programmes. Most of them will be concerned with purely library techniques but occasionally there is something relevant to information skills teaching. In schools in-service training is often available but there may be difficulty in non-teaching staff being allowed on the courses. In special libraries, it depends very much on the type of organization in which the library or information unit is placed. If it is an education-slanted organization the opportunities are usually good, if it is commercially-based then they may be few.

Acquiring teaching techniques outside the organization brings in the question of fees and time. If both are unlimited (extremely unlikely) the possibilities are endless. If both are severely limited (extremely likely), the opportunities are few. The professional bodies of the library and information world offer an enormous range of courses, seminars, meetings, etc but although they are sometimes cheap, they are not too often practically-orientated and they generally deal with professional matters and continuing professional education.

Chapter Fifteen

Relevant literature

Introduction
Throughout the text of this book a deliberate attempt has been made to offer practical advice to you who are working in the small library or information unit and who might want to set up a programme of teaching information skills. Supporting evidence for the approach taken or acknowledgement of assistance has been included only where it is necessary or illuminating, so the very minimum of references to the extensive literature on information skills teaching has been made.

In the chapter on cooperation, however, the value to you of outside support was emphasized, in particular the need to draw on the experience and expertise of your counterparts in similar situations. Some of this experience and expertise has been committed to print, and consequently it would be very remiss of me not to include a selection of the most relevant literature. Theoretical papers which do not relate their ideas to practical situations are generally avoided, and preference has been given to papers describing practice. These may sometimes be mundane, unexceptional and unadventurous, but they reflect real circumstances, perhaps not dissimilar to yours.

Most of the papers (with the exception of some of those dealing with schools and colleges) deal predominantly with the library skills elements of information skills. The current (it is not entirely new) conception of information skills is only barely reflected in the literature as yet, so the text of the present book will have to redress the balance.

For the most part the literature has been drawn from the UK. This seems only sensible with the schools and colleges sectors, because the literature on information skills from other countries (notably the USA) draws on situations and circumstances which are often too closely dependent on their different educational systems and backgrounds. In the case of public and special libraries, some overseas references have been included partly because the educational background is not prominent nor significant, but also partly because the UK literature is relatively small.

These references should not be regarded as containing models of good or bad practice, but as illustrations of tried practice — so be discriminating.

Schools

Information skills in the current interpretation are most fully illustrated in the literature dealing with schools. Because of this one or two general papers on information skills training are included here. For the most part, however, the following papers and reports describe information skills training in specific schools in the UK. Many of the authors of these case studies are teachers, and they discuss and illustrate their approach to information skills training frequently in the context of a curriculum subject like geography, history, chemistry, etc.

They display a wide variety of approaches to information skills training, but even then you may not find a programme which can fit your school. Yet you may see possibilities from several different papers through which you may be able to develop your own programme. In either case you can be sure that there is no 'package' which you can simply slot into your school.

1 *Information skills in the secondary curriculum: the recommendations of a working group sponsored by the British Library and the Schools Council.* Edited by M Marland. London, Methuen Educational for the Schools Council, 1981.

> The development of information skills presents difficulties both for teachers, who may have problems assessing which skills they require students to use, and for students, who are often not given the opportunity to practise a balanced range of skills. The purpose of this report is to help schools plan a curriculum policy around information skills — the ability to formulate

and focus a question, find possible sources, judge their appropriateness, extract the relevant information, reorganize it, and prepare it for future use or presentation to others — in short, to encourage and assist students to organize their learning during school and beyond. The working group, by dissecting an apparently simple assignment, identifies a series of stages (nine 'question' steps) which students need to work through. These stages are examined, and ways in which teachers might stimulate the development of the necessary study skills are discussed, together with their relationship to the overall curriculum. The report recommends a whole-school policy, firmly rooted in the underlying curriculum plans of the school, absorbed into departmental syllabuses and thence into classroom assignments. Although the emphasis is on information and study skills within the secondary school, all teachers and librarians will find useful guidance. A valuable appendix to the report is a set of detailed guidelines for a workshop for staff to prompt a re-appraisal of the skills demanded in assignments.

2 Barton, T and Barton, N 'Study skills in geography teaching' in *Starting to teach study skills.* Edited by A Irving. London, Arnold, 1982, 48-61.

This paper covers the practice of teaching geography study skills at Stanney County Comprehensive School and Brookvale County Comprehensive School. The context in which these skills are taught is initially outlined for both schools, then the authors concentrate on their approach to teaching the skill of using an atlas and interpreting a variety of maps. This is taught by means of worksheets and these are illustrated throughout the text.

3 Brake, Terence *The need to know: teaching the importance of information. Final Report for the period January 1978 — March 1979.* London, British Library Board, 1980. (BLR&DD Report No 5511)

The aims, history, rationale and development of *The need to know* — community information in schools project — are outlined and discussed; the project was placed in the context of the needs of the pupils of South Hackney Secondary School in particular, and of inner-city children in general. The project was primarily an exploratory one and data were gathered largely by participant observation in the school, supplemented by questionnaires and interviews with staff and pupils. Details of the collection and organization of community information for the school are described, particularly in relation to the 'information needs' of the pupils. The largest section of the report is given over to a description and evaluation of the trial 10-week teaching programme, which aimed to teach fourth-year pupils the importance and use of community information in the management of everyday problems. Some of the teaching materials produced are presented in appendices to this report. The report emphasizes that *The need to know* must not be seen as an isolated phenomenon that can be simply slotted into existing social education programmes; the roots of the project lie not in social education as such but in the developing area of information skills. In this context *The need to know* would be seen as the culmination of a long educational process — based upon the principle of learning to learn — and not a fragment to be patched onto the curriculum before the pupils leave school. Schools wishing to teach such programmes should first formulate whole school policies towards the teaching of information/study skills.

4 Coles, M H, Shepherd, C A and White, C 'The science of library and book skills'. *School librarian* 30 (3) 1982. 200-207.

The authors (three teachers) believe that science has as important a role as any other major curriculum subject in developing children's reading and study skills. Science is a particularly useful context for the development of successful reading strategies, book skills and project work. Examples of teaching materials to develop these skills are given from lower-school science but the principles can be applied throughout the age range. The strategies involved in these various skills are described, in particular those concerned with project work. The authors suggest that pupils should have a checklist of the various stages of the project (produced as a bookmark). They also provide for teachers a diagrammatic check-list for planning project work.

5 Herring, J 'User education in schools: purposes, problems, potentials'. *School librarian* 28 1980. 341-345.

The author identifies the main purposes of user education in schools as firstly, locating material and information in the library, and secondly, using the material and information found (described as study skills and information-handling skills). Locational skills should be taught in the context of the subjects studied, and the information and study skills need to be taught in relation to curricular work as a whole. A balance of both sets of skills needs to be taught. He then goes on to consider the problem of teaching these skills in school (particularly the integration of user education with the curriculum), and suggests the approach that might be taken — communication between teachers and librarian, forming groups between them, drawing up programmes, etc. Finally, the potential of user education is considered, with reference to computers, less gifted children and their use of information after leaving school, and sixth-formers going forward to higher education.

6 Lake, B 'English teaching and study skills' in *Starting to teach study skills*. Edited by A Irving. London, Arnold, 1982. 16-28.

Although the school in question (Romsey School, Somerset) has a study skills programme operating during pastoral time, there is a study skills programme appropriate to the English lesson which complements this. The programme is described. The approach is to make study skills an integral, but at the same time, an identifiably separate feature of the syllabus. Two features which ensure that the pupils take greater responsibility for their own learning and thus their independence are the primacy of talk and mutual aid, and these are outlined first. The author begins with the skills of talking, listening and observing, and how the pupils learn these skills. He then goes on to describe the teaching of ten fundamental thinking activities necessary in many areas of the secondary curriculum — observing, identifying similarity, grouping, summarizing, translating, judging, assuming, inventing, researching and hypothesizing. In each case the skill is discussed, the activity in the class that develops this skill is described, and other possible related activities are suggested.

7 Lindsay, J 'Information training in secondary schools'. *Education libraries bulletin* 19 (3) 1976. 16-21.
An experiment in training students at South Hackney School, London, in information handling skills is described. The various skills necessary for each year are described and discussed. The programme is also intended to introduce students to information sources outside school, those relevant to living problems.

8 Swindells, A P 'The school library: its place in the school and its use as a teaching centre'. *Essex education* March 1965. 247-248.
The teacher-librarian at Loughton Fairmead County Secondary School describes the library's involvement with teaching at the school. The paper concentrates on topic work with the children in the library. It involves careful planning between the teacher-librarian and the teacher before the projects are begun, and close cooperation between both as the children work on their assignments. The topic work in the library is illustrated by work in geography and history (one teacher actually does all her history teaching in the library).

9 Trigg, S 'The use of the library'. *School librarian* 29 (4) 1981. 302-306.
An educationalist outlines what is required in a library skills programme. He divides the programme into location skills (orientation to the library and its organization) and evaluation skills (including reading skills, note-taking, information evaluation, etc). The latter should be taught in close liaison with subject teachers, he argues.

10 White, C and Coles, M 'Libraries and laboratories'. *School librarian* 28 (3) 1980. 237-242.

The authors call for a model of library instruction where the development of library skills should be determined by the type of work undertaken in the school. The pupils would begin this work through the medium of a particular subject, and then, for example, books would be analysed and evaluated for the relevant information they contain. They advocate the acquisition of library skills through the discipline of science and outline ways in which the library can be utilized as an important resource supporting the science curriculum. The authors illustrate their approach with an example of one of their Science Library Survival Packs.

Colleges

The literature on colleges illustrates the potential for the teaching of information skills as part of TEC, BEC, etc courses. The modules so far largely centre on library skills and not perhaps sufficiently on other information skills.

The other main stimulus for information skills instruction is the project and one or two case studies are selected for inclusion here. This is only part of a substantial number of papers on this theme.

1 Bradley, P 'Library involvement in syllabus panels' *Information and library manager* 2 (4) 1983. 112-113.

The author initially discusses library instruction in college libraries in the UK and identifies three distinct kinds of such teaching. He concentrates on classes which are an assessed part of a course, usually as part of a General Studies paper, and in particular the courses in the syllabus validated by SCOTEC in the colleges in Scotland. The aims of one of these syllabuses (OND in Building, 1979-80) are presented in full.

2 Finn, D, Ashby, M and Drury, S *A teaching manual for tutor-librarians*. London, Library Association, 1978.

This is a teaching manual designed for use by tutor-librarians in a variety of college libraries. It aims to be practical and contains suggestions, examples of work already taking place in libraries, exercises and specimens of examination papers. Methods of planning and developing courses, ideas for content are given. It includes proposals for all types of student, from Liberal Studies students to secretarial students. Publicity methods for the college library and the instruction courses are included.

3 Library Association, Colleges of Further and Higher Education Group *Examples in library work for TEC and BEC courses.* Library Association Colleges of Further and Higher Education Group, 1980.

This draws together a few examples of library work for TEC and BEC courses. The aims and outlines of the courses are given in full. They cover the use of library materials, report writing, citing references and literature searching. Examples of exercises and projects are given. Comments on the courses are made.

4 Library Association, Colleges of Technology and Further Education Section Committee 'Outline syllabus for BEC and TEC modules for non-librarianship students'. *CTFE bulletin* (22) Summer 1978. 10-12.

The Committee of the Colleges of Technology and Further Education Section of the Library Association drew up recommended course outlines for use in colleges of further and higher education in the UK. These outlines (one to the Business Education Council and one to the Technican Education Council) are presented here.

5 McElroy, A R and McNaughton, F C 'A project-based approach to the use of biological literature'. *Journal of biological education* 13 1979. 52-57.

A course is described which has been designed to increase students' ability and willingness to use and read the scientific literature, and ultimately to enable them to make their own contributions to the literature in an acceptable style and format. The objectives and methods of the course differ from those of traditional library-use courses by concentrating on making students read and evaluate the literature rather than on information retrieval per se. Reactions have been favourable. Students make more and better use of the literature and the standard of presentation of written work was improved. The work habits generated by the course assist students throughout their academic careers.

6 Nettlefold, B 'A course in communication and information retrieval for undergraduate biologists' *Journal of biological education* 9 1975. 201-205.

To help biology students cope with the growth in the number of information sources in the life sciences a compulsory course in 'Communication and information retrieval' was introduced into the BSc degree in Biology at Paisley College of Technology. The course is outlined together with some discussion of its advantages and disadvantages.

7 Scanlan, G M, Harding, J V and Redfearn, D S 'The library project as part of a national certificate course' *Vocational aspect of secondary and further education* 13 1961. 141-145.

The metallurgy and engineering students at Wandsworth Technical College are encouraged to make use of library materials other than standard text-books by means of project work. They make use of information from other sources as well as the college library and the resulting work was of a very high standard.

Public libraries
The literature on public libraries includes many case studies of programmes for a variety of groups, but mainly schoolchildren and adults involved in adult education courses. They are almost all fairly unambitious, looking to improve the use and exploitation of the public library's service rather than to teach information skills techniques in the widest sense, for example, evaluation of information sources, communication skills, etc. This applies even to those libraries which have programmes associated with schools or adult education.

1 Foster, A 'You look in the librarian's drawers, miss!' – Sheffield City Libraries School Instruction Service' in *Library Association, Study School and National Conference*

Proceedings. Nottingham, 1979. London, Library Association, 1980. 76-79.

The objectives of the Sheffield City Libraries School Instruction Service are to show children that libraries are interesting, to show them the materials available, to give them some insight into the arrangement and use of books and to give them confidence in using the library. To achieve these objectives children are invited to the library and given tours and instructions. All schools in Sheffield, including special schools, are encouraged to use the service. Details of its use are given.

2 Hendley, M 'The librarian as teacher: research skills for library patrons at Kitchener Public Library'. *Ontario public review* 63 (1) 1979. 45-48.

Following courses organized by local universities at Kitchener Public Library which attracted the general public, it was noted that adults were asking assistance in researching topics. The library consequently decided to arrange a series of research skills workshops. These are described, along with the advertising campaign promoting the workshops.

3 Kahn, C F 'The public library and adult education' *ALA Adult Services Division newsletter*, 7 Fall 1969. 11.

The author outlines the ways in which Passaic County Learning Center has incorporated instruction in the use of the library into an Adult Basic Education programme which deals with newly-literate adults.

4 Rogers, M L 'Library project with teachers in training' *Top of the news* 18 1961. 19-24.

The Oberlin College Library, in conjunction with the public library and a school librarian, ran a summer course of teaching materials instruction for student teachers. The course is outlined together with a brief look at developments in successive years.

5 Scrivener, R 'User education in public libraries — a practical exercise' in *Second International Conference on Library User Education, Keble College Oxford, 7-10 July 1981.*

Proceedings. Edited by P Fox. Loughborough, INFUSE Publications, 1982. 60-66.

> The why, how and what of Woodbridge Public Library's 'Know your library better' course for adults is fully described. The place of such courses in the public library sector is discussed. An appendix gives the content and timetable for the course.

6 Sleath, C 'Learning about libraries course, Norwich Central Library' *INFUSE* 5 (1) 1981. 11-12.

> Six-session courses on learning about libraries, organized by Norwich Central Library, are described. They were run as continuing adult education courses under the aegis of the Adult Education Centre in Norwich. The content of the courses reflects two aims: to give information about the workings of libraries so that course students could become more self-sufficient as users; and to demonstrate the variety and extensiveness of the materials available in the library.

Special libraries
Without doubt, information skills teaching in the special library sector is difficult, and this is apparent both in the lack of literature on the subject and the content of the papers that have described it. In fact there is barely a handful of papers which describe programmes in this sector, and you are left with a few papers which indicate the approaches that might be taken, while stopping short of illustrating the approach by a working example.

1 Brookes, A 'Some user education techniques appropriate to special libraries'. *Australian Special Libraries news* 13 (1) 1980. 15-18.

> This suggests that orientation and bibliographic instruction are unsuitable to special libraries. Instead, three activities — promotion, education and training — serve as a better framework for user education. Promotion is a form of public relations. Education concerns informing people about the library and its resources and this includes library guides, library tours, signs and bibliographies. Training is the actual teaching of people to use the library resources efficiently. All the sug-

gestions made under each heading are briefly described and are seen as a basis for a user education programme.

2 Lakie, M H 'User education in industrial libraries: needs, benefits, techniques' in *Third International Conference on User Education, University of Edinburgh, 19-22 July 1983. Proceedings.* Edited by P Fox and I Malley. Loughborough, INFUSE Publications, 1983, 48-55.
   The paper proposes that appropriate and far-reaching changes in management attitudes to library provision in industry may be effected through a four-level programme of user education. The first three levels are chiefly concerned with how to find items in a particular library. The fourth level (aimed at members of the management team) includes developing awareness of the potential and actual contribution of the library to achieving departmental and organizational objectives.

3 Malley, I 'Educating the special library user'. *Aslib proceedings* 30 (10-11) 1978. 365-372.
   The argument for user education in special libraries is presented. The case for on-line searching is discussed. Illustrations are drawn from the fields of medicine and the construction industry to support the argument that information awareness is the tactic most appropriate for the special library sector in developing information skills.

4 Orna, E 'Should we educate our users?' *Aslib proceedings* 30 (4) 1978, 130-141.
   The author discusses the role of the information service provided by special libraries in organizations. Thorough understanding of the particular organization, how it functions and its purpose is recommended in order that the library users' needs can be understood. The benefits to any organization of an effective information service are outlined.

5 Swan, H 'Development of user education in a technical library' in *Current R & D projects in user education in the UK. Proceedings of a conference held at Loughborough*

University of Technology, 22 March 1979. Edited by
I Malley. Loughborough, INFUSE Publications, 1979,
C1-C14.

The background material for the conference presents
the results of a sample survey of staff use of the Uni-
lever Research Library at Colworth and their reactions
to library instruction. A copy of the questionnaire is
provided. The main requirements emerging from the
survey are for guided library tours, better subject
markings, a fixed display of instructions on how to
find various items, increased signposting and problem
sheets on the use of the library. The author briefly
outlines plans for the tours and a better display system
as requested by the library users.

Index